Architizer

Architizer
The World's Best Architecture

Φ

Letter from the Founder

Architecture is universal—most people living on Earth spend their lives surrounded by buildings. This is why the A+Awards are judged by everyone. Traditional architecture awards too often consist of architects telling other architects what great architecture is. The A+Awards differ in this aspect: they are a forum for the voices of architecture's consumers. We are all consumers of architecture, and these are our awards.

It is my pleasure to present you with the winners of the 2018 A+Awards.

—Marc Kushner

Amazing Architecture— as Chosen by You

For too long, architecture has been intertwined with exclusivity. Prestigious industry awards are typically given out to star architects, presenting individual geniuses as the face of the profession. Oftentimes, the winners of these awards are chosen by a small group of fellow architects, each with his or her own agendas and historical biases. Surely, this system leaves out the most important opinions of all— those of the people who live, work, and play inside buildings every day.

Architizer's A+Awards, the world's largest awards program for architecture and building products, is dedicated to changing this prevalent imbalance. Launched in 2013, its design democracy attracts public votes from multiple hundred thousand users, giving a true picture of what outstanding architecture looks like today. The program's aim is not to create more starchitects. Instead, it gives the spotlight to entire design teams and the structures they work so hard to create. Architecture has never been an individual pursuit, and the A+Awards strive to demonstrate the power of great teamwork and collaboration. More importantly, the projects that follow illustrate the essential ingredients of amazing buildings, defined not by architecture's "inner circle," but by everyone who uses and participates in the creation of the built environment.

To this end, there are two types of A+Award given for each category. Winners of the Popular Choice Awards are chosen by the global public using an online voting system. Additionally, the Jurors' Awards are selected by a group of more than four hundred visionary practitioners from the world of design, technology, fashion, business, and more. These experts understand the power of stellar architecture to enrich global communities, while at the same time forming a community diverse enough to assemble balanced and fair results—a true reflection of exemplary design.

To ensure all types of architecture firms can be recognized for their work, the A+Awards are split into a wide range of categories across three broad groups. Firstly, the Typology categories celebrate traditional building types, ranging from residential, office, and commercial to transportation, landscape, and cultural structures. Secondly, the Plus categories are designed to showcase how architects build relationships, celebrating the intersection of architecture with lighting, art, communication, technology, and others. Finally, the Product categories reward the spectacular products and materials that help make architects' visions a reality.

What, then, do the winning projects tell us about the state of contemporary design? While the projects in this book are incredibly diverse—both in terms of geography and typology— they share certain traits that elevate them from being simply good to being truly exceptional. As hand-picked examples in a gallery of innovation and creativity, these buildings are united by common factors that today's architects are striving to perfect.

First and foremost, materiality is key. Rojkind Arquitectos' Foro Boca Concert Hall in Mexico is a glorious ode to concrete, composed of monumental blocks that echo the rocky edge of the surrounding seawall. Steven Holl Architects' Maggie's Center in London is an urban lantern of translucent polycarbonate that glows softly each evening, emanating a comforting warmth that uniquely benefits its inhabitants. Meanwhile, H&P Architects' aptly named Brick Cave in Đông Anh, Vietnam, is a house wrapped in a veil of perforated bricks, creating a shaded interior sprinkled with dappled light.

The architects behind each of these magical spaces harnessed raw materials in a way that celebrates their unique properties, requiring no covering up or hiding away. There is a great sense of honesty embedded within these buildings—plasterboard, cornicing, and stucco are eschewed, allowing each material to be showcased in a way that inhabitants can instantly recognize and appreciate. This expressive approach to architecture can only be achieved through impeccable detailing, which in turn necessitates a high level of craftsmanship—another trend running through the projects in this book.

For evidence, one can look to Heatherwick Studio's extraordinary transformation of grain silos for the Zeitz Museum of Contemporary African Art in Cape Town. The project's stunning faceted glazing was carefully conceived by the design team, expertly manufactured by Mazor Aluminum, and then gently slotted into the concrete shell. Similarly, the charred timber shingles of META-Project's Stage of Forest—a stunning retreat in the snowy hills of Changchun, China— were meticulously wrapped around the cantilevered shell of the building to form an extraordinary outlook onto Songhua Lake. Then, there is Luigi Rosselli Architects' Beehive in Australia's Surry Hills, its facade shrouded with a rhythmic veil of reclaimed terra-cotta tiles that mediate the sun and the wind.

In each of these cases, the collaboration between architects, fabricators, and builders was essential to the project's success. A single, carefully considered junction between two elements can make all the difference—look for where contrasting floor finishes meet, where tiles converge on a hipped roof, or where a door slides seamlessly into a wall. These key details form powerful examples of exactly that synergy between designers and construction teams that can be found throughout this book.

Beyond beautiful materiality and clever detailing, many winning projects also demonstrate the power of program to improve the lives of communities in need. ZAV Architects utilized innovative sandbag construction to create the Rong Cultural Center, a crucial gathering place for the people of Hormuz Island in Iran. In a very different environment, Matthew Mazzotta created another joyful social catalyst in the shape of the Storefront Theater in Lyons, Nebraska, formed by a shop facade that converts into seating and a stage for local performances. These projects illustrate the potential for architecture to bring people of all backgrounds together, while also proving that transformative design need not cost the Earth.

Of course, for every successful completed building, there are a dozen or more innovative conceptual projects that are yet to be constructed. For this reason, unbuilt designs are also celebrated by the A+Awards, with each rendering, sketch, or model representing ideas that are as influential as many finished structures. These ideas range in scale from the intimate—think PARA Project's Pioneertown House, nestled among boulders in a Californian desert—to the epic, like Coldefy & Associés Architectes Urbanistes' Tropicalia, the world's largest tropical greenhouse under a single dome. They are projects that provoke us to think about how we experience space. They spark the imagination by offering up exciting visions for futures to come.

Even with these unbuilt projects, a whole host of talent is involved, from architects and designers to rendering artists and model makers. Together, they help to make the abstract tangible, just as manufacturers and builders do with completed structures. This synergy ties back to the core purpose of the A+Awards. Rather than glorifying a single project author, the award-winning buildings in this book are a testament to the incredible teamwork needed to bring an architectural project from concept to completion.

When successfully combined, a team's collective abilities can result in buildings that transcend pure functionality and become inspiring beyond their own matter. The best architecture may be crafted from concrete, glass, wood, and stone, but when it all comes together, it amounts to so much more: it is a social condenser, an atmospheric cauldron, a visual delight. It is a spirit lifter, an educator, a calming influence, and, maybe, a home.

Each of the projects within this book is all of these things and more. Together, they make for better cities and improve the lives of those who inhabit them. It is the power of good architecture to perform ordinary tasks exceptionally well. Chosen by you, these projects stand to define what good architecture is.

—Paul Keskeys
Managing Editor, Architizer

Jury and Popular Choice Winners

Station F—1,000 Startup Campus
Paris, France
Wilmotte & Associés SAS

The Halle Freyssinet is a large shed, originally used for the shipment of goods, built in the late 1920s by the French engineer Eugène Freyssinet. This remarkable building in prestressed reinforced concrete is located in the urban renewal area of the Paris Rive Gauche mixed development area. Preserving, restoring, and modernizing this rough-cast concrete umbrella was a real challenge; an innovative technique for applying concrete was used to provide the shed with an exceptionally slender load-bearing structure.

It was necessary to add new energy systems to the historic building, to break its isolated location by including two public passages through it, to provide space for three thousand workstations, and to introduce new significant architectural elements.

The former Halle Freyssinet now houses STATION F, a start-up campus, which is a workplace that gathers all services required for entrepreneurial and digital creation activities. It aims to create a greater coherence in a start-up ecosystem that was previously fragmented. STATION F is made up of three distinct zones: the Share forum for digital sharing and interaction, the Create zone in the center of the shed dedicated to start-up work spaces, and the Chill zone, which will host a 37,700-square-foot (3,500 square meters) restaurant.

TYPE
COMMERCIAL:
COWORKING SPACE

WINNER
JURY

PROJECT STATUS
BUILT

YEAR
2017

FIRM LOCATION
PARIS
FRANCE

Sanbaopeng LKKER Jingdezhen Ceramic Design Center
Jingdezhen, China
Office Mass

TYPE
COMMERCIAL:
COWORKING SPACE

WINNER
POPULAR CHOICE

PROJECT STATUS
BUILT

YEAR
2018

FIRM LOCATION
SHANGHAI
CHINA

Sanbaopeng LKKER Jingdezhen Ceramic Design Center is located on a slope in Sanbao valley in Jingdezhen, China, with a stream running through it. The architects intended to make use of the original natural environment around the site to inspire the designers, as well as enable the space itself to build a deep connection with ceramic art.

Sagger is a type of utensil that has been used since the Song dynasty to shape porcelain while producing ceramics. The Ceramic Design Center is designed as a giant sagger containing the contemporary design innovations and traditional craft of porcelain.

The circular sagger floats above the stream, providing a panoramic view outward. The floor of the building follows the fluctuation of the terrain, and the interior space is naturally separated into two parts on different elevations. They are connected with two wide stairs, bearing the possibility to be used as a meeting and exhibition area.

The facade of the building is made of a screenlike copper tile system that controls the interior lighting, while the constantly rusting copper provides a saggerlike color and texture.

Martin's Lane Winery
Kelowna, BC, Canada

Olson Kundig

The design of this Kelowna, Canada, winery is a direct response to the French Pinot Noir grape often cultivated here. Overhandling the *must*, or wine juice, can quickly diminish the quality of Pinot Noir wine. As such, the client's wine-making philosophy designated that Martin's Lane Winery be based on a gravity-flow process in order to minimize any manipulation of the Pinot Noir *must*.

The production facility answers this need for a gravity-flow process with a tiered design that steps down its steeply sloped, lakeside site. Utilizing the downhill grade, the functional areas of the building begin with the grape-receiving area at the top, through fermentation and the settling room, down to the bottling room, and finally to the below-ground barrel storage area.

While the production area closely follows the contours of the land, the hospitality portion is distinguished by a dramatic split in the building.

Cantilevering out over the vineyard below, the design of this visitor area expresses a second response to the hilly setting—one based on the prospect and the views of nearby Lake Okanagan. Clerestory and operable windows in the seam of the building maximize daylight and natural ventilation by capturing lake breezes as they rise up the hill.

TYPE
COMMERCIAL:
FACTORIES & WAREHOUSES

WINNER
JURY

PROJECT STATUS
BUILT

YEAR
2016

FIRM LOCATION
SEATTLE, WA
USA

TYPE
COMMERCIAL:
FACTORIES & WAREHOUSES

WINNER
POPULAR CHOICE

PROJECT STATUS
BUILT

YEAR
2017

FIRM LOCATION
SKOPJE
MACEDONIA

Factory for Bottling Natural Water MAYA
Gari, Macedonia

Aleksandar Karangelov Architecture Studio

The factory MAYA produces bottled water and is located in an isolated mountain area in Western Macedonia. Simply speaking, the design is composed of two cubes touching one another. One is the production plant, and the other is the administration and accommodation block. Several open or semiopen areas throughout the building provide spaces for relaxed employee breaks. The production plant has an area of 53,820 square feet (5,000 square meters), while the administration and accommodation block occupies an area of 12,900 square feet (1,200 square meters).

The entrance hall is extended throughout all the floors; it changes direction but follows the main horizontal and vertical communications, creating a fluid space without borders. The entrance connects to the outside through big glass curtain walls, echoing the production hall. These two areas plug into the energy and the spirit of the location to narrate the main idea of this project: connecting the inside with the outside. It forms a human place to work by distinguishing itself from the classic definition of inside and outside as rigorously separate entities. The building is free of any borders and uniformity and embraces transparency while aiming to complement the natural surroundings.

Chaoyang Park Plaza
Beijing, China

MAD Architects

Having a similar position and function as Central Park in Manhattan— but unlike the surrounding modern boxlike buildings that only create a separation between the park and the city—Chaoyang Park Plaza is an expansion of nature. It is an extension of the park into the city, naturalizing the CBD's strong artificial skyline, borrowing scenery from a distant landscape—a classical approach to Chinese garden architecture, in which nature and architecture blend into one another. The asymmetrical twin tower office buildings on the north side of the site sit at the base of the park's lake and are like two mountain peaks growing out of the water.

The small-scale, low-rise commercial buildings appear like mountain rocks that have endured long-term erosion. They seem to be randomly placed, but their strategic relationship to one another forms a secluded, yet open urban garden, constituting a place where people can meet within nature in the middle of the city.

The two multistory Armani apartments to the southwest continue this concept of open-air living with their staggered balconies, offering each residential unit more opportunities to be exposed to natural sunlight and ultimately feel a closeness to nature unusual in cityscapes.

TYPE
COMMERCIAL:
MIXED USE

WINNER
JURY

PROJECT STATUS
BUILT

YEAR
2017

FIRM LOCATION
BEIJING
CHINA

Empire Stores
Brooklyn, NY, USA

STUDIO V Architecture,
S9, and Perkins Eastman

Once referred to as *Fortress Brooklyn*, Empire Stores acted as a barricade between the residential neighborhood and the dangerous working waterfront. Today the storage warehouse is the gateway to Brooklyn Bridge Park and the waterfront. The original masonry exterior, schist structural walls, and timber-frame construction define its adaptive reuse, which reflects the new culture of Brooklyn.

The design for Empire Stores is an homage to the original aesthetic of the warehouse and its nineteenth-century structures inspired by three sources: first, the dramatic dual expanse of the Brooklyn and Manhattan Bridges as they slice through the fabric of the city;

second, the *Carcieri* drawings of Piranesi that imagined towering voids bisected by vertical bridges and staircases; and third, the Anarchitecture of artist and architect Gordon Matta-Clark. Brought together, these sources of inspiration create a tension between interior and exterior.

Empire Stores has welcomed a new mix of tenants from the technology, media, retail, hospitality, and cultural sectors, exchanging its industrial heritage for a creative future. The vertical courtyard carves out a social space in thebuilding while simultaneously displaying the energy and activity of its creative businesses.

TYPE
COMMERCIAL: MIXED USE

CONCEPTS — PLUS ARCHITECTURE + RENOVATION

WINNER
POPULAR CHOICE

PROJECT STATUS
BUILT

YEAR
2017

FIRM LOCATION
NEW YORK, NY
USA

Abu Dhabi National Oil
Company Headquarters
Abu Dhabi, United Arab Emirates

HOK

The headquarters of the Abu Dhabi National Oil Company (ADNOC) represent this state-owned institution as a pillar of the UAE's economy. ADNOC's elegant, minimalist design stands out to express stability, strength, and seriousness of purpose. The exterior frame of the seventy-five-story tower is clad in granite to convey a sense of permanence.

To provide the ideal solar orientation, HOK designed the headquarters in the shape of a parallelogram. The tower's north side, facing the waterfront, is fully glazed to offer views and take advantage of the limited direct sunlight. Columns are located twenty feet (six meters) from the northern perimeter, allowing the structure to be cantilevered from this side and create unencumbered interior space.

The south side—where the sunlight is stronger—incorporates a double wall of insulated, fritted glass and sunshades. Granite cladding on the east and west sides screens the sixty-five-story glass core from harsh sunlight. Especially fitted high-efficiency fixtures, the reuse of graywater, and HVAC condensation reduce potable water use by 40 percent. More than one thousand gallons (3,785 liters) of graywater per month are harvested and recycled for flushing toilets and watering plants. It is hoped that these strategies will help to achieve LEED Gold certification.

TYPE
COMMERCIAL:
OFFICE — HIGH-RISE
(16+ FLOORS)

WINNER
JURY

PROJECT STATUS
BUILT

YEAR
2016

FIRM LOCATION
WASHINGTON, D.C.
USA

Lè Architecture
Taipei, Taiwan

Aedas

The design for Taipei Lè Architecture draws inspiration from the shape of river pebbles. It has a unique aesthetic that conveys softness and elegance next to strength and character. Located in close proximity to the Jilong River, the surrounding environment provided the architects with the opportunity to propose a building that has the potential to redefine the skyline of this rapidly developing district.

The eighteen-story office building is conceived of as an incubator of knowledge, where innovative ideas are seeded and turned to reality. The rounded silhouette of the north and south facades tapers gradually as it rises higher. The enclosed curtain wall harmonizes with the outer structure by creating a series of outdoor balconies offering unparalleled views for the users.

The office space is planned to provide a highly efficient, yet healthy and inspiring work environment. A cantilevered communal space incorporates pantries, coffee shops, libraries, and brainstorming areas. These amenities are weaved together to provide an urban fabric akin to a living room, and aim to promote creativity and catalyze interactions between office users.

TYPE
COMMERCIAL:
OFFICE — HIGH-RISE
(16+ FLOORS)

WINNER
POPULAR CHOICE

PROJECT STATUS
BUILT

YEAR
2016

FIRM LOCATION
HONG KONG

Chongqing Sunac One Central Mansion Sales Pavilion
Chongqing, China
AOE

TYPE
COMMERCIAL:
OFFICE — LOW-RISE
(1-4 FLOORS)

WINNER
JURY

PROJECT STATUS
BUILT

YEAR
2017

FIRM LOCATION
BEIJING
CHINA

Based on the client's stipulation, this sales office will be converted into a kindergarten after its initial use. The architects' strategy was to add a layer of removable green skin of metal mesh outside the building for sustainability and image purposes. This layer of skin creates a unique facade. The Chinese-style wood structure emphasizes the expression of an architectural logic following the laws of nature.

Structural components such as pillars, beams, brackets, rafters, and purlins are all exposed, complying with a natural look. The overhangs of the eaves form a gray space, thus creating a vague zone that merges views of nature and building to achieve a symbiotic state between man and nature. Further, the use of metal fabric for the secondary skin results in a sustainable curtain that protects the building from direct sunlight to save energy.

The internal and external spaces are linked visually and spatially by a graceful transition. Translucent materials—exposing a looming visual blur—convey a rich level of depth in space. Together, the translucency and the elegant landscape create a poetic, zenlike space. Although the architectural form and the materials are modern, the core idea is grounded in the tradition of Chinese architectural philosophy.

The Beehive
Sydney, Australia

Raffaello Rosselli Architect
and Luigi Rosselli Architects

The Beehive explores how an undervalued waste product, such as the ubiquitous terra-cotta roof tile, can be redefined and revalued.

Located in the center of Sydney, Australia, the project features recycled tiles that have been built into a complex rhythmic sunshade that mediates the sun and wind. The facade design was largely conceived through multiple full-scale tests and hand-built prototypes, opening up a tactile process of rapid prototyping and experimentation. Each tile course is placed based on its function. The acute course was used at the bottom due to its strength, as well to obscure the solid spandrels. Equilateral tiles were used at eye level to reduce visual obstructions, while diagonal tiles were used at the top due to their low clearance.

Challenging the generic and often alienating nature of open-plan office buildings, the design sought to provide an active but intimate environment with multiple working positions. The main space is defined by two linear rows of semienclosed booths, linked by a long, linear standing bench, which facilitates collaborative work.

On the top floor, a communal garden terrace offers a point of release to work in the sunshine, hold community events, or relax after a long day. Below this level, the conference table is partially enclosed by a terra-cotta tile bookshelf.

TYPE
COMMERCIAL:
OFFICE — LOW-RISE
(1-4 FLOORS)

DETAILS — PLUS:
ARCHITECTURE + FACADES

WINNER
JURY
POPULAR CHOICE

PROJECT STATUS
BUILT

YEAR
2017

FIRM LOCATION
SYDNEY
AUSTRALIA

Baltyk
Poznan, Poland
MVRDV

MVRDV's design for Baltyk, its first project in Poland, responds to the site's historic location, which is of particular importance for Poznan—the site of the old Baltyk cinema, from which the project lends its name. Located on Rondo Kaponiera, at a major intersection next to Poznan's central train station, and the main highway leading to the city's airport, Baltyk is a new landmark mixed-use contemporary building for the city. It includes a 129,160-square-foot (12,000 square meters) office space, an 8,000-square-foot (750 square meters) panorama restaurant, 14,530 square feet (1,350 square meters) of retail space in the plinth of the building, and three levels of underground parking. The building benefits from the close vicinity of a hotel, the restored Concordia printing house, a new creative center for business, and the MTP international exhibition building. The flexible office building is limited to a depth of twenty-three feet (seven meters), allowing daylight to generously penetrate the work spaces. Toward the south, a slope of cascading patios offers outdoor spaces to the users of the building.

Its overall mass follows the maximum volume and height restriction of the site. The result is an unusual form, which appears completely different depending on the angle from which it is approached.

TYPE
COMMERCIAL:
OFFICE — MID-RISE
(5–15 FLOORS)

WINNER
JURY

PROJECT STATUS
BUILT

YEAR
2017

FIRM LOCATION
ROTTERDAM
THE NETHERLANDS

7 St. Thomas
Toronto, ON, Canada

Hariri Pontarini Architects
and Guardian Glass

The 7 St. Thomas project harmonizes retail and commercial design through an inventive interplay of form and light, blending Victorian and contemporary materials to create a unified appearance. Six heritage town houses have been integrated into a three-story podium, extending into a sinuous six-story tower above. The development houses retail at ground level and condominium office spaces throughout, blending attractive design, ecological responsibility, and civic enhancement.

Located around the corner from the busy Bay Bloor intersection, the design was born from a desire to seamlessly integrate into the fabric of the neighborhood and to contribute to the urban environment. The building peels back from the neighboring context to preserve the light and views of existing residential buildings.

The podium wraps around and incorporates the heritage buildings by matching them in scale and proportion, using glass and stone to contrast with and enhance the existing facades. The tower is wrapped in fritted glass and undulates in response to the urban fabric of the site, allowing for light penetration. The contrast between the solidity of the red-brick heritage houses below and the translucent permeability of the glass tower—which steps back and floats above the Victorian frontages—highlights both typologies.

TYPE
COMMERCIAL:
OFFICE — MID-RISE
(5–15 FLOORS)

DETAILS — PLUS:
ARCHITECTURE + GLASS

WINNER
JURY
POPULAR CHOICE

PROJECT STATUS
BUILT

YEAR
2017

FIRM LOCATIONS
TORONTO, ON
CANADA

CARLETON, MI
USA

Crossboundaries Office
Beijing, China

Crossboundaries

Architecture firm Crossboundaries' contemporary studio took its initial form from a 1950s auditorium.

With the spread of rapid, raze-and-rebuild development in contemporary China, older buildings are becoming increasingly rare, especially in trendy areas like Sanlitun in Beijing. Crossboundaries used a plug-in approach to bring four new office spaces into the former auditorium, creating a new relationship by involving the existing building and its history.

The four offices for independent lease are centered around the double-height, lofty atrium, ideal for coworking and events. A new roof with evenly scattered skylights is raised above the original roofline, making room for mezzanine

levels above each office and bringing ample natural daylight into the space. The mezzanine level is freestanding and stepped back from the original outer walls, forming voids for circulation, air, and filtered natural light.

Crossboundaries occupies the office at the end of the atrium. Upon arrival, the principal floor is a large, open space that can be utilized for meetings, reception, and community events, with the mezzanine level operating as the primary work space. A service area at the back of the office is anchored to the existing auditorium wall, serving as a kitchen and storage space, and featuring a small meeting room on the ground floor.

TYPE
COMMERCIAL:
OFFICE INTERIORS
(<25,000 SQ. FT.)

WINNER
JURY

PROJECT STATUS
BUILT

YEAR
2015

FIRM LOCATION
BEIJING
CHINA

Private Jewelry Retail Office #4
Tehran, Iran

CAAT Studio

The project is a jewelry showroom for a client who needed a unique space. The problem that the architects had to solve was to give a new definition to a jewelry retail office/showroom in a small space, namely a 754-square-foot (seventy square meters) apartment unit located in Tehran's grand bazaar.

Naturally, project users are divided into two groups: customers and staff. How these two groups communicate with each other was the subject of CAAT Studio's design. Customers do not necessarily need to have visual contact between one another, but the staff must constantly communicate with each other.

The solution was to divide the space into two parts. Firstly, all extra parts of the existing space were demolished to create a stage with a single theme using a monotone color palette. Secondly, the architects used material variation as a way of bringing contrast to the environment while maintaining the integrity of the design. The jewelry showroom and trade area were located in the center, pushing the management and entrance zone to the perimeter of the unit. The display counter encapsulates four independent customer zones unified by a curvy design program.

TYPE
COMMERCIAL:
OFFICE INTERIORS
(<25,000 SQ. FT.)

WINNER
POPULAR CHOICE

PROJECT STATUS
BUILT

YEAR
2018

FIRM LOCATION
TEHRAN
IRAN

Pinterest HQ2
San Francisco, CA, USA

IwamotoScott Architecture
and Brereton Architects

TYPE
COMMERCIAL:
OFFICE INTERIORS
(<25,000 SQ. FT.)

WINNER
JURY
POPULAR CHOICE

PROJECT STATUS
BUILT

YEAR
2018

FIRM LOCATION
SAN FRANCISCO, CA
USA

This new Pinterest headquarters, occupying a new 150,000-square-foot (13,935 square meters), six-story concrete structure in San Francisco's SoMa district, is positioned to create an urban campus, along with the company's earlier work spaces completed down the street. The main lobby at ground level constitutes one of the city's privately owned public open spaces (POPOS). It is glassed in, but has an operable corner that opens to a newly landscaped midblock alleyway. Within this double-height lobby, the architects designed a café called the Point that is run by Pinterest. Similar to the earlier HQ design, a bespoke wood ceiling along Brannan Street and custom built-in furniture is

put in place to act as a superthreshold between Pinterest and the city.

The all-hands dining space occupies most of the second floor. A communication stair connecting this level to all upper floors switches back and hangs from the ceiling as a sculptural object animating the POPOS below. The stair forms a linear cascade for the upper four floors. A porous band of meeting spaces, detailed with intersecting glass corners, becomes a spatio-programmatic filter between the stair, core, and perimeter workstations. Thus, the stair acts as the central organizing figure to the work space.

The Conversation Plinth is the first hardwood-cross-laminated-timber (HCLT) structure constructed in the United States Its form takes cues from the conversation pit found in the iconic Miller Home, as well as the plinths that elevate the landmarks immediately surrounding the site— the library designed by I. M. Pei, the First Christian Church designed by Eliel Saarinen, and the Large Arch by Henry Moore. The installation offers a place for the community to gather and converse.

Although softwood CLT already existed, HCLT did not. The plinth is constructed from the first ever commercial pressing of HCLT in America, an effort led by IKD using mixed-species, low-value hardwoods.

The installation is intended to be a catalyst for a new timber industry by up-cycling low-value hardwoods that are extracted from regional forests. HCLT offers numerous benefits over softwood, included superior mechanical properties, material volume savings, and increased resistance to fire, among others.

By demonstrating the viability and the benefits of a new, high-value timber market in the Midwest, the project has the potential to initiate a cascade of effects: job growth in rural forestry and manufacturing, diversifying hardwood lumber markets, higher land value, and improved forest management practices to reduce wildfires and encourage biodiversity.

TYPE
COMMERCIAL:
POP-UPS & TEMPORARY

WINNER
JURY
POPULAR CHOICE

PROJECT STATUS
BUILT

YEAR
2017

FIRM LOCATION
BOSTON, MA
USA

Conversation Plinth:
Indiana Hardwood CLT Project
Columbus, IN, USA

IKD

Cheese Tart Shop BAKE
Ho Chi Minh City, Vietnam

07Beach

This project was designed to be the first shop of the Japanese cheese tart brand BAKE in Vietnam. To utilize the property's character—which has a double-height ceiling and faces a street—the stairs from the entrance to the cashier were put in place to show passersby that customers queue in a vertical direction. This resulted in each tart display table appearing to be stairlike. The interior also features a sloping floor.

The client required an open, highly visible interior without optical barriers between staff and customers. In computer renderings, different lightnesses were applied to each surface to emphasize the shade of an object. The same method was then used during the construction, applying lighter colors on horizontal lines and darker colors on vertical surfaces. The lighter shades were also applied to walls in the staff area, thereby highlighting the area as if it were a stage.

Displaying their tarts to passersby was important for BAKE—the store's floor level was, however, higher than the street. Due to this difference in level, a stairlike mirrored ceiling was designed to reflect the tarts outward to the street, making them easily visible to potential customers.

TYPE
COMMERCIAL:
RETAIL

WINNER
JURY
POPULAR CHOICE

PROJECT STATUS
BUILT

YEAR
2017

FIRM LOCATION
KYOTO
JAPAN

CityLife Shopping District
Milan, Italy
Zaha Hadid Architects

Located above Tre Torri station on the M5 line of Milan's metro network, CityLife Shopping District integrates a new public park with indoor and outdoor piazzas, a food hall, restaurants, cafés, shops, and a cinema, as well as facilities for health and well-being.

The 344,430-square-foot (52,000 square meters) shopping district will welcome seven million visitors each year when the CityLife redevelopment is fully completed in 2020. CityLife is one of Europe's largest redevelopment projects and will include one thousand new homes, offices for almost ten thousand staff, the new forty-two-acre (seventeen hectares) park, piazzas, and a kindergarten.

Bamboo flooring, ceiling, and columns welcome visitors to the shopping district's interior. Selected for its warmth and tactility, engineered bamboo is extremely durable and can be procured in a large quantity from sustainable sources.

The solidity of the bamboo floor and columns meets the louvered bamboo ceiling at the capitals of each column, expressing a unity between the solid and porous surfaces. Assembled with resins under high pressure, engineered bamboo blocks were carved by five-axis CNC milling and hand finished to create the shopping district's interior columns, capitals, and counters.

TYPE
COMMERCIAL:
SHOPPING CENTER

WINNER
JURY

PROJECT STATUS
BUILT

YEAR
2017

FIRM LOCATION
LONDON
UK

Mega Foodwalk
Samut Prakan Province, Thailand

FOS (Foundry of Space)

TYPE
COMMERCIAL:
SHOPPING CENTER

WINNER
POPULAR CHOICE

PROJECT STATUS
BUILT

YEAR
2017

FIRM LOCATION
PHAYATHAI
THAILAND

The Mega Bangna Shopping Complex is as big as a small town. Its central building is perceived as a downtown, whereas the Foodwalk zone on the east wing has green areas and canals. The new Retail zone extension, located on the eastern periphery, beyond the existing zone, could be conceptualized as a valley. The layout of the new open-air mall is composed around a central courtyard space in which a sunken plaza with an amphitheater acts as the main social space for gathering.

Continuing from the sunken plaza on the bottom level, the sloping green area in the middle of the layout, called the Hill, ascends to connect with the existing Mega Plaza on level one. The Hill is intended to be a relaxing space where people can immerse themselves in the lush landscape. By embedding greenery into the courtyard and throughout the building, the project becomes a hybrid between a marketplace and a public park where social interactions are encouraged.

Colormix Store
São Paulo, Brazil
Basiches Arquitetos Associados

TYPE
COMMERCIAL:
SHOWROOMS

WINNER
JURY
POPULAR CHOICE

PROJECT STATUS
BUILT

YEAR
2017

FIRM LOCATION
SÃO PAULO
BRAZIL

Located in São Paulo, Brazil, on a traditional street that contains a great number of architecture and interior shops, Colormix Store is focused on selling internal and external coatings for buildings.

Together with the client, Basiches Arquitetos Associados designed a unique material for the entire facade: a triangular-shaped skin, internally structured by metal sheets and covered in marblelike porcelain tiles. It references the specific purpose of the shop, which offers a particular service of cutting and splicing porcelain pieces to produce imperceptible joints.

The concept for the interior design included the creation of two very distinct spaces. On the ground floor, products are exhibited on walls following an elaborate layout and adopting the character of an art gallery. The floor has been put together using tiles with graphics created by the plastic artist and photographer Flavio Samelo.

On the upper floor, there is a more traditional showroom with several display showcases. Natural lighting contributes to the comfort of the interior. On the ground floor, there are two openings to the outside.

The use of a single white material on the facade connotes the image of a monolith. The openings, and the displacement between pavements, create a set of fillings and voids that are reinforced by a special lighting program at night.

TYPE
COMMERCIAL:
UNBUILT COMMERCIAL

WINNER
JURY

PROJECT STATUS
CONCEPT

YEAR
2018

FIRM LOCATION
CHICAGO, IL
USA

Kolos Data Center
Ballengen, Norway

HDR

Located in Ballengen, Norway, Kolos's 6.5 million-square-foot (six hundred thousand square meters) and four-story data center is designed to take advantage of the country's competitive green energy systems, cool climate, and large technical workforce.

As a response to its site located on a fjord, surrounded by mountains and integrated into the natural beauty of its environment, the design takes cues from the spectacular landforms of alluvial fans, mountains, and glaciers that define the area. Organized along a central spine, the buildings's forms are arranged to mimic glacial movement as it displaces swaths of land. At the base, the spine creates a collision of landforms reinterpreted to become modular data halls that are secure, scalable, and connected.

At the terminus on the water, the central spine emerges as a public element clad in copper—a reference to the area's copper mining history. This architectural gesture articulates the entrance to the data center while acting as a gateway to the public waterfront promenade.

The massive climate-cooled facility, powered by Norway's abundant hydropower, has the potential to scale beyond one thousand megawatts of computing power to service the rapidly growing global data market.

No. 5

Beirut, Lebanon

BAD. Built by Associative Data

TYPE
COMMERCIAL:
UNBUILT COMMERCIAL

WINNER
POPULAR CHOICE

PROJECT STATUS
CONCEPT

YEAR
2018

FIRM LOCATION
BEIRUT
LEBANON

Located in the heart of the Jnah district in Beirut, the mixed-use project No. 5 organizes 161,460 square feet (15,000 square meters) of residential apartments and offices over a two-story retail plinth in a compact urban form.

Nestled in an L-shaped site at a busy junction, the development creates an attractive public space sheltered from surrounding traffic, forming a new focal point for the high-density restaurant, retail, office, and residential environment. The building volume is

shaped as an extrusion of the site, creating a sharp edge to the chaotic urban fabric around it. Carved out of this solid volume is a contrasting soft public space with a series of terraces and courtyards. This new public space allows maximized exposure of the program at ground level while also increasing natural daylight and inviting ventilation for offices and residential apartments.

Using computational tools and modeling, the massing was studied

under various programmatic and environmental parameters to optimize the building's footprint. Its pixelated volume works to enhance the environmental strategy to create a comfortable external public space by allowing controlled wind infiltration and solar radiation.

Limestone Gallery
Guizhou Province, China
3andwich Design and He Wei Studio

Surrounded by Karst Canyon, the Anlong Limestone Resort is located in Guizhou Province, China, covering about seven hundred acres (283 hectares). The Limestone Gallery sits on a cliff over 525 feet (160 meters) high from which one can overlook the entire canyon. The design fully respects the local culture and its natural environment in terms of modern architectural language. By implementing public and artistic programs to the resort, the design is regarded as a showplace that connects the village with the outer environment.

The total floor area of the Limestone Gallery measures 8,600 square feet (eight hundred square meters) with two floors inside, including an exhibition, conference, and service area. The rooftop is used for sightseeing, while the bottom floor is designed as an outdoor lounge and outdoor venue for exhibitions and performances. As a result of variations in topography, and the existence of unstable giant rocks, the shape of the building resembles an asymmetrical crescent.

The Limestone Gallery's facade is designed with a curved glass wall, creating a magnificent panoramic view over Haiwei canyon. The highlighted horizontal lines of the facade reinforce the relationship between the building and the rock. Meanwhile, the glass texture helps to communicate this context by setting its fluid transparency in contrast to the rigid mountains.

TYPE
CULTURAL:
GALLERY

WINNER
JURY

PROJECT STATUS
BUILT

YEAR
2017

FIRM LOCATION
BEIJING
CHINA

MiG-1.0
Quito, Ecuador
odD+

MiG-1.0 is a mobile inflatable gallery, which can be placed in countless different contexts. Without dismantling, MiG-1.0 deflates and folds into its mobile container, ready for its next stop. This multipurpose, lightweight structure is essentially a transportable venue with the purpose of housing different events and exhibitions.

The structure is made 95 percent from recycled and reused materials. The "hard space" is an upgraded recycled container clad with exhibition panels made from particle board. The "soft space," or inflatable area, is made 100 percent from recycled billboards. These spheres are modular and can grow horizontally depending on the material exhibited inside. Recycled tire flooring modules were used for the hard floor inside the spherical exhibition space.

TYPE
COMMERCIAL:
RETAIL

WINNER
POPULAR CHOICE

PROJECT STATUS
BUILT

YEAR
2015

FIRM LOCATION
QUITO
ECUADOR

Chapman University Musco Center for the Arts
Orange, CA, USA
Pfeiffer

The design for the Chapman College Musco Center for the Arts met the challenges of height restrictions, conformity to the campus architectural vernacular, and budget through scale, siting, and material.

The architecture, landscaping, and interiors all draw inspiration from the concept of a Renaissance garden. The new plaza, recalling the former sunken lawn that stood before Memorial Hall, will host outdoor productions, further establishing the cultural core of the campus. Due to height limitations, the site was excavated to accommodate a strong axial approach. The building is fronted by a grand archway and flanked asymmetrically by four majestic columns. Through these pillars, one enters the enclosed "garden" of the lobby, a gathering space that looks outward, with exterior balconies overlooking the plaza and amphitheater.

The design for the interior of the audience chamber, which supports both symphonic music and the dramatic arts by means of a one-of-a-kind fully flown orchestra shell, was inspired by the secret garden, or *ragnaia*. The complex acoustic requirements were resolved by a reinterpretation of the multiple layers of the acanthus plant as large abstract petal-shaped wall panels, building on the *ragnaia* concept and wrapping the rich copper palette into the woven wire ceiling elements.

TYPE
CULTURAL:
HALL / THEATER

WINNER
JURY

PROJECT STATUS
BUILT

YEAR
2016

FIRM LOCATION
LOS ANGELES, CA
USA

Lotte Concert Hall
Seoul, South Korea

Kohn Pedersen Fox Associates

TYPE
CULTURAL:
HALL / THEATER

WINNER
POPULAR CHOICE

PROJECT STATUS
BUILT

YEAR
2016

FIRM LOCATION
NEW YORK, NY
USA

A full-sized, classical performance venue seating more than two thousand people, the Lotte Concert Hall is located on the roof of the Lotte World Mall.

The concert hall is the first new venue of its kind in Seoul, South Korea, in the last twenty-five years, and it has been recognized as one of the foremost classical performance venues in Asia, featuring world-class acoustics and sumptuous interiors. Designed in the vineyard style—referencing its terraced appearance—the seating completely surrounds the stage to provide the audience with an immersive experience.

The swelling form of the Lotte Concert Hall is a reaction to the curves that surround it—the subtle lines of the tower, the "scoop" of public plaza below, and the rounded corners of the adjacent cinema tower.

Vibration control emerged as a major design challenge for the hall, given its location on top of another structure, which itself is adjacent to one of the city's metro lines. A box-in-a-box system—completely separating the internal structure of the concert hall (floor, walls, and ceiling) from the external structure—emerged as the most viable solution for eliminating outside vibration and noise.

Zeitz MOCAA
Cape Town, South Africa

Heatherwick Studio

Zeitz MOCAA is the first major museum in Africa dedicated to contemporary art from the continent and its diaspora.

Originally built in the 1920s, by 2001 the silo had fallen into disuse, and while the rest of the surrounding harbor became regenerated into a place of leisure and tourism, the silo was in need of a new purpose. Heatherwick Studio developed a concept to transform the silo's tightly packed concrete cellular structure into a new museum with spaces suitable for displaying art while retaining its industrial heritage.

To connect the two major parts of the complex, a 108-foot-tall (thirty-three meters) storage annex consisting of forty-two vertical concrete tubes and a 108-foot-tall (thirty-three meters) grain elevator tower were carved out of a central atrium from the silo's cellular structure.

Modeled on a grain of corn, the atrium's shape was scaled up to fill the volume of the storage annex and translated into thousands of coordinates.

The seven-inch-thick (170 milimeters) concrete tubes were lined with inner sleeves of reinforced concrete following the desired atrium shape. Together, all sleeved tubes formed a gigantic arch spanning the future atrium space and provided a cutting guide for removing portions of the old silos. The remaining internal tubes were removed to make space for eighty white-cube gallery spaces.

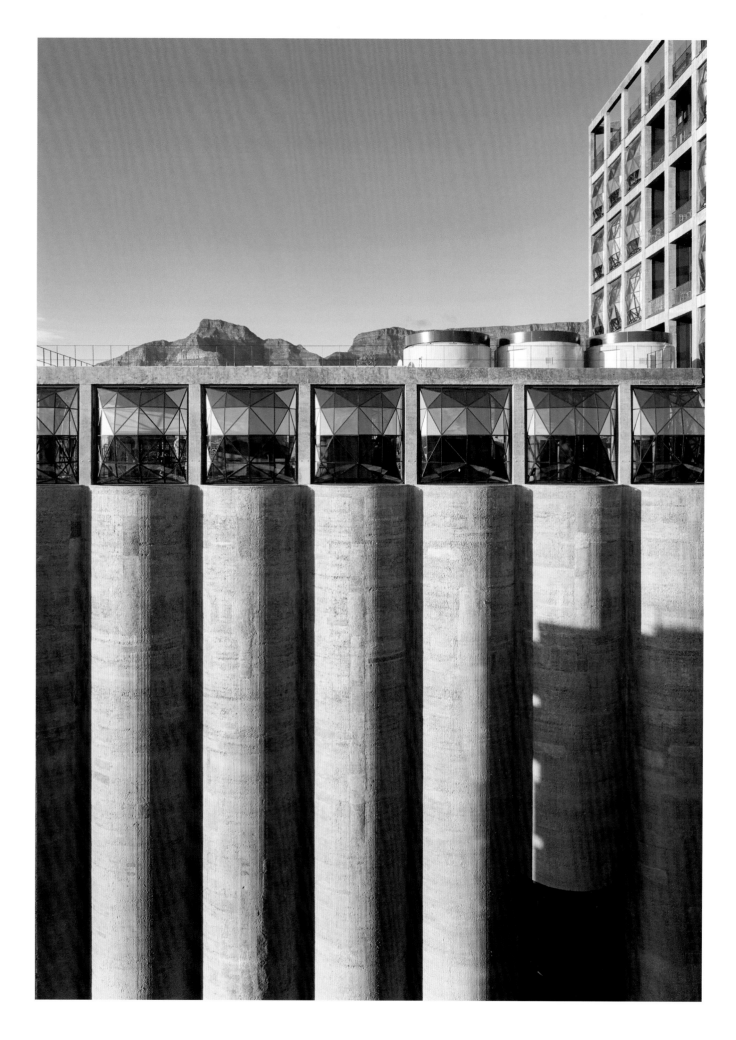

TYPE
CULTURAL:
MUSEUM

WINNER
JURY

PROJECT STATUS
BUILT

YEAR
2017

FIRM LOCATION
LONDON
UK

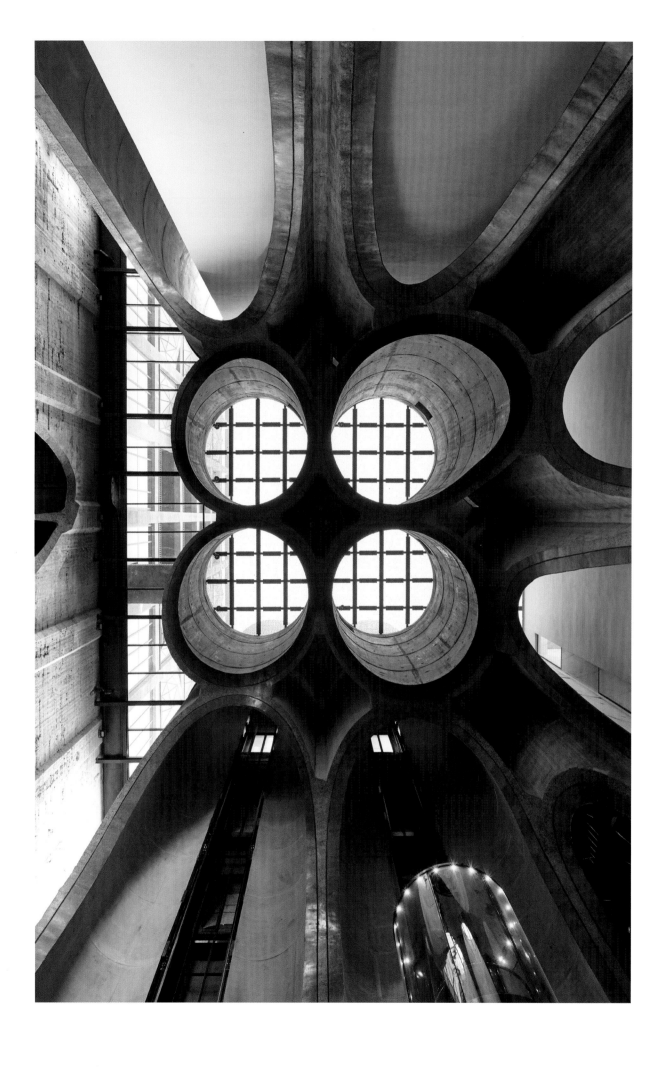

Museo Del Prado en Filipinas
Manila, Philippines

WTA Architecture + Design Studio

TYPE
CULTURAL:
MUSEUM

WINNER
POPULAR CHOICE

PROJECT STATUS
BUILT

YEAR
2017

FIRM LOCATION
SAN JUAN
PHILIPPINES

The Museo del Prado en Filipinas consists of sixty paintings housed in thirty portable modules built at a total cost of seven thousand dollars. It seeks to reimagine a museum as an engaging, barrier-free, and localized place. The deconstructed program breaks down the idea of a museum into three basic components: shelter, viewing space, and exhibition space.

The separate modules celebrate the vaults and arches of the Museo del Prado in Madrid; each module consists of a display space held up by a pair of bended steel arches that form the frame for a billowing taffeta sail. This harkens back to the visiting galleons that tied Manila to Spain and allowed the designers to give the museum a volume that provides shelter for visitors and filters the sunlight.

The modules were arranged to re-create various viewing situations in a museum, such as corridors, galleries, and centerpieces. By bringing the museum to the people, it liberates culture from traditional monolithic institutions and the pilgrimage needed to visit them.

The Prado is an inclusive museum open to all. The street kids run along its corridors, and people who would never think of going to a museum suddenly find themselves face-to-face with art.

Confluence Park
San Antonio, TX, USA

Lake|Flato Architects and Matsys Design

Confluence Park is an intricate teaching tool that allows visitors to gain a greater understanding of the ecotypes of the South Texas region and the function of the San Antonio River watershed. Located at the confluence of the San Antonio River and San Pedro Creek, the idea of confluence is ingrained in every aspect, from gestures like the landform of the park representing the convergence of ecotypes in the South Texas region to the pavilion petals imitating the form of native plants.

Constructed of concrete petals designed to sit lightly upon the land, the BHP Pavilion forms a geometry that collects and funnels rainwater into an underground storage tank. The pavilion provides shade and shelter, engaging visitors to simultaneously visualize the cycle of water at Confluence Park and how it relates directly to the San Antonio Rivershed. The multipurpose Estella Avery Education Center, featuring a green roof that provides thermal mass for passive heating and cooling, serves as a classroom space that opens to the pavilion. Rainwater collected through a site-wide water catchment system serves as the primary source of water throughout the park, and the entire site is powered by a photovoltaic array designed to provide 100 percent of on-site energy on a yearly basis.

TYPE
CULTURAL:
PAVILIONS

WINNER
JURY

PROJECT STATUS
BUILT

YEAR
2018

FIRM LOCATIONS
SAN ANTONIO, TX
USA

OAKLAND, CA
USA

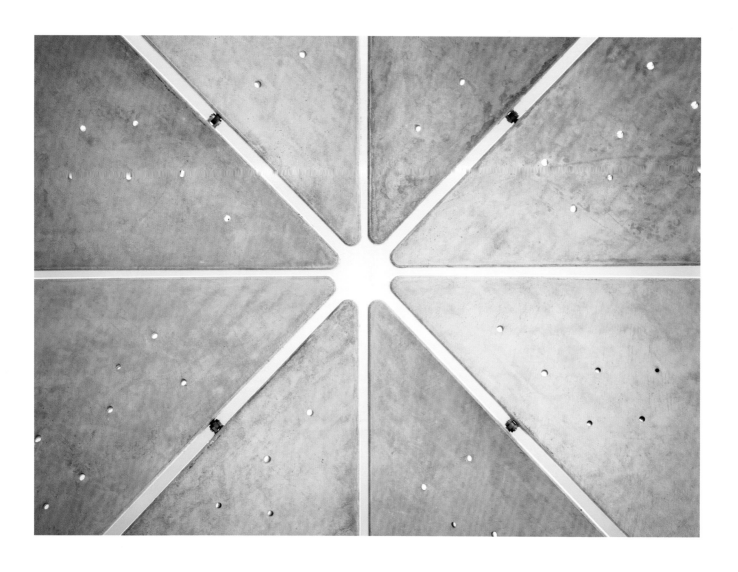

Stage of Forest
Jilin, China
META-Project

TYPE
CULTURAL:
PAVILIONS

DETAILS — PLUS
ARCHITECTURE + WOOD

WINNER
POPULAR CHOICE

PROJECT STATUS
BUILT

YEAR
2017

FIRM LOCATION
BEIJING
CHINA

Stage of Forest is situated on a hillside between a forest and a slope. The site is surrounded by luscious greenery in summer and covered by an overwhelming amount of white snow in winter. The location and triangular shape of the stage was determined after precise examination of the site conditions.

As one descends from the mountaintop, the structure slowly rises above the undulating landscape. The entire stage uses charred cedar shingles cladding to form a dialogue with the Mongolian oak forest and its surrounding mountains and valleys.

The building combined rough materiality with sensuous forms. Seen from afar, the stage is a dark, free-floating monolith in the landscape. On coming closer, the reflection on the charred cedar shingles becomes faintly perceptible. When one finally arrives at the platform level, a great panoramic view of the Songhua Lake opens itself up to the viewer's eyes. The red cedar plank wall has been left untreated and is vivid in color shades, in contrast to the building's dark wood exterior. In this project, different treatments of wood are introduced as a binding agent between nature and people.

Capela de Nossa Senhora de Fátima
Idanha-a-Nova, Portugal

Plano Humano Arquitectos

TYPE
CULTURAL:
RELIGIOUS BUILDINGS
& MEMORIALS

DETAILS — PLUS
ARCHITECTURE + WOOD

WINNER
JURY
POPULAR CHOICE

PROJECT STATUS
BUILT

YEAR
2018

FIRM LOCATION
LISBON
PORTUGAL

This building took shape from the desire to have a chapel at the National Scout's Activities Camp in Idanha-a-Nova, a municipality in Central Portugal. It sits atop a plateau, surrounded by a rural environment with an extraordinary panoramic view. The chapel is dedicated to Our Lady of Fátima and is inspired by the scouting experience: outdoor life, camping, tents. The pointy edges of the building allude to the scout's scarf, the near-global symbol of commitment to this movement.

The east-west orientation enables the sunrise to illuminate its interior space, and the sunset to fill the place with colors, tones, and ambiences. The large cross, with its imposing and yet delicate form, tapers as it gains height and testifies to the solemnity of the place.

The wood-and-zinc structure gives a simple and protective external aspect to the temple, and creates a cozy interior ambience. Inside, the covering is supported by twelve wooden beams revealing the constructive simplicity. With a total length of forty feet (twelve meters), the structure reaches its highest point at thirty feet (nine meters), after the altar, where the raising of the main beam increases the space's depth and highlights this sacral point.

United Kingdom Holocaust Memorial International Design Competition Entry
London, UK

Diamond Schmitt Architects

TYPE
CULTURAL:
UNBUILT CULTURAL

WINNER
JURY

PROJECT STATUS
CONCEPT

YEAR
2018

FIRM LOCATION
TORONTO, ON
CANADA

In the United Kingdom, an international design competition for a National Holocaust Memorial was held to honor the victims and survivors of the Holocaust and Nazi persecution. The memorial's proposed site is in Victoria Tower Gardens, alongside the Houses of Parliament and adjacent to the River Thames.

The subtlety of the design gradually reveals the power of the opposing forces that created the descent into a horror of hitherto unimaginable scale, and a humanity of unlimited compassion and selfless commitment.

The proposal centers around two themes: immeasurable loss and emptiness, represented in a design that is a void in the landscape—the presence of absence—and, secondly, the journey from light to darkness and vice versa. This represents the descent from discrimination to destruction and a reverse of utter despair into hope.

Circling the heart of the memorial, the gently sloped helical ramp takes visitors past a recitation of the names of the most notorious death and concentration camps. The cast-iron walls of the enclosure are textured with a bas-relief of six million small rectangular nuggets, providing some comprehension of the magnitude of the Holocaust's toll.

Museum of Forest Finn Culture
Svullrya, Norway

Lipinski Lasovsky Johansson

TYPE
CULTURAL:
UNBUILT CULTURAL

WINNER
POPULAR CHOICE

PROJECT STATUS
CONCEPT

YEAR
2017

FIRM LOCATION
COPENHAGEN
DENMARK

Surrounded by an array of columns, the project evokes curiosity and attracts visitors to interact with the building and the surrounding landscape. The museum creates a framework to present and educate about the rich history of the Forest Finns (Finnish migrants who settled in forested areas of Norway during the late sixteenth century), and it is characterized by the large roof and the forest of columns creating a symbiosis between nature and building. The playful column facade creates a unique expression, especially during dark hours when light from inside trickles through the column forest and lightens up the surrounding landscape.

When one approaches the building, the entrance appears as a glade through the forest, leading into the reception area, café, and library. Once one is inside the museum, the columns are still present and light is filtered through the ceiling—a reference to a building technique by the Forest Finns whereby smoke was ventilated out through a smoke hatch. The museum is a simple building that in many ways relates to Forest Finn culture and its direct relation to the forest. Wood is present in both structural elements and interior spaces, where, for example, burnt wood tells a story about the slash-and-burn cultivation in Forest Finn culture.

:PM Club
Sofia, Bulgaria
Studio Mode

:PM club is and always will be a temple of music. As some may say: "Come pray in the temple and your sins will be kept secret. Consciously you will follow the path to the altar where the almighty DJ greets and embraces you with the sound of music. Experience darkness, light, and infinity."

The nightclub is located on the ground level of a hotel building built in 1962. The complicated space was shaped and organized by the architects, who experienced a number of technical setbacks. The footprint of the main hall formed a perfect square, which is said to be the most difficult shape for space organization. Creating and assembling the ceiling cupola with a diameter of twenty-eight feet (nine meters), Studio Mode pushed and extended its technical and engineering abilities toward altitudes yet unknown.

In the main hall, the architects placed the dome right above the bar, thus instantly creating the heart of the club. The result of the space and Studio Mode's aesthetic approach is a foyer where up is down and vice versa, and a main music hall where light, sound, and the materialization of ideas become one in moments of infinity.

TYPE
HOSPITALITY:
BARS & NIGHTCLUBS

WINNER
JURY
POPULAR CHOICE

PROJECT STATUS
BUILT

YEAR
2017

FIRM LOCATION
SOFIA
BULGARIA

Maggie's Centre Barts
London, UK
Steven Holl Architects

TYPE
HOSPITALITY:
HEALTH CARE & WELLNESS

WINNER
JURY

PROJECT STATUS
BUILT

YEAR
2017

FIRM LOCATION
NEW YORK, NY
USA

Maggie's Centre Barts is the latest facility for Maggie's Centres, an organization that provides practical, emotional, and social support to cancer patients and their families. The center sits in central London adjacent to St Bartholomew's Hospital, founded in the twelfth century.

While most of the realized Maggie's Centres have been horizontal buildings, the historically charged site required a vertical structure. The building was envisioned as a "vessel within a vessel within a vessel." The structure is a

branching concrete frame, the inner layer is perforated bamboo, and the outer layer is matte-white glass with colored glass fragments recalling notation of medieval music of the thirteenth century. The outer glass layer is organized in horizontal bands like a musical staff, while the concrete structure branches like the hand.

The three-story center has an open curved staircase integral to the concrete frame with open spaces vertically lined in perforated bamboo. There is

a second entry to the west, opening to the garden of the adjacent church. The building tops out in a public roof garden with flowering trees open to a large room for yoga, Tai Chi, and meetings.

Wellness Plesnik
Logar Valley, Slovenia

Enota

Hotel Plesnik is a boutique family hotel in the heart of a park in the Logar Valley, Slovenia. Its exceptional location at the end of this glacial valley offers an unforgettable view of the Alp's majestic peaks.

Much of the space of the preexisting wellness center was originally taken up by a small, organically shaped pool, opening onto a tanning deck directly in front of the building. To recover space needed for new programs, the pool was in part replaced by a large whirlpool, while a section of the former pool shell (closer to the view of the valley) was repurposed as a sunken circular resting area with a fireplace. The sun deck has been extended to include a natural swimming pool, which makes up for the eliminated interior water surface, while the water's reflection further accentuates the view.

Despite natural filtration by means of aquatic plants, the new pool is rectilinear in shape and designed to be a continuation of the building, not the surrounding landscape. To reference the interior resting area and its fireplace, a relaxation area featuring a fire ring has been placed in the middle of the water surface outside.

TYPE
HOSPITALITY:
HEALTH CARE & WELLNESS

WINNER
POPULAR CHOICE

PROJECT STATUS
BUILT

YEAR
2017

FIRM LOCATION
LJUBLJANA
SLOVENIA

Pierhouse and
1 Hotel Brooklyn Bridge
Brooklyn, NY, USA

Marvel Architects

It is a project that outnumbers many others: Pierhouse comprises 106 condominium units, a below-grade parking garage for three hundred cars, a seventeen-thousand-square-foot (1,580 square meters) event space, and a 195-key hotel in a 550,000-square-foot (51,100 square meters) complex of connected buildings ranging from four to ten stories.

Pierhouse performs as an extension of Brooklyn Bridge Park—a verdant backdrop recalling the high, sandy bank of precolonial Brooklyn Heights, screening urban noise while facilitating waterfront access.

The building presents two faces: the west elevation cascades toward the park, while the east elevation rises steeply from Furman Street, responding to the urban fabric of narrow streets and a nearby expressway. This Janus condition informs two distinct facades, innovative residential floor plans, and skip-stop circulation. The residential buildings employ a repeating module of distinct duplex houses with terraces on the park and harbor views. Their double-height interior spaces and multilevel plans reinterpret the classic Brooklyn brownstone in a multifamily structure.

Starwood Capital Group's 1 Hotel Brooklyn Bridge is an urban threshold to the park with a forty-foot-tall (twelve meters) public plaza, double-height lobby, outdoor dining, event spaces with glass walls opening directly on the park, and roof terrace drawing the park and its visitors into the building. The project will achieve LEED Silver certification.

TYPE
HOSPITALITY:
HOTELS & RESORTS

WINNER
JURY

PROJECT STATUS
BUILT

YEAR
2016

FIRM LOCATION
NEW YORK, NY
USA

Bailixiangju Resort
Beijing, China

Spear Designs and Spacework Architects

TYPE
HOSPITALITY:
HOTELS & RESORTS

WINNER
POPULAR CHOICE

PROJECT STATUS
BUILT

YEAR
2017

FIRM LOCATION
BEIJING
CHINA

What is to be done with China's seven hundred thousand left behind villages? How can the leisure demands of hundreds of millions of newly affluent consumers be met?

Spear Designs and Spacework Architects started with these questions when challenged to transform Dashiyao, a mountain village that had been emptied by government order and whose population had been relocated to newly built row houses up the valley.

Charged with respecting the ambience of the original village, the architects modified existing buildings and judiciously added new construction. The existing facades and tile roofs of Dashiyao's farmhouses were retained,

while new brick buildings with dark gray standing seam aluminum roofs add a crisp contemporary note to the resort.

At the center of the complex, what had been the village hall and primary school was insulated and painted in a luminous sky blue. Now part of a five-fingered public area, these buildings were repurposed as the resort's activity center and restaurant.

The village of Dashiyao has been gently and thoughtfully reimagined: it is now a delightfully engaging, highly functional and efficient resort of 50,310 square feet (4,674 square meters) on fifty-four acres (twenty-two hectares) of landscaped grounds.

Noma 2.0
Copenhagen, Denmark

BIG—Bjarke Ingels Group
and Studio David Thulstrup

TYPE
HOSPITALITY:
RESTAURANTS

WINNER
JURY
POPULAR CHOICE

PROJECT STATUS
BUILT

YEAR
2018

FIRM LOCATIONS
BROOKLYN, NY
USA

COPENHAGEN
DENMARK

Situated between two lakes and within the community of Christiania, Denmark, Noma 2.0 is built on the site of a protected ex-military warehouse once used to store mines for the Royal Danish Navy. The restaurant is imagined as an intimate garden village, and guests are welcomed to experience a new menu and philosophy that will redefine Noma for years to come.

For the new Noma 2.0, a collaboration between architectural firm Bjarke Ingels Group and interior design firm

Studio David Thulstrup, the restaurant's individual components were first identified, then collected into a new gourmet village. A total of eleven spaces, each tailored to a specific need and built of the finest materials best situated for their functions, are densely clustered around the restaurant's heart: the kitchen.

Noma 2.0 takes visitors on an odyssey through a variety of Nordic materials and building techniques. Every hut within the village is constructed with

the finest materials: the giant walk-in barbecue hut features cast iron; the kitchen is designed like a panopticon with an oversized hood hovering over the chefs; and the lounge looks and feels like a giant, cozy fireplace made entirely of brick. The new gourmet village sits in the middle of an urban farm where many of the ingredients are grown and bred.

Alila Wuzhen
Xizha, China

GOA

Alila Wuzhen is two miles (three kilometers) from the well-known Xizha tourist area in China. It is a land of idyllic beauty and an oasis of serenity amid chaos.

The hotel boasts a building area of 270,840 square feet (25,162 square meters) with 126 villa-type suites. Its overall pattern takes villages south of the Yangtze River as its prototype, retaining the spatial forms, basic elements, scales, and colors. The tranquil water surface and pure architectural form are well coordinated and perfectly reflect the multilevel and semitransparent relations between buildings, plants, and water surface.

The architects explored the possibility of traditional space reconstruction and endowed streets, lanes, courtyards, and other spatial types with a new function and spirit. Meanwhile, the well-proportioned spaces full of twists and turns—usually seen in traditional settlements—are still present in this project.

TYPE
HOSPITALITY:
UNBUILT HOSPITALITY

WINNER
JURY

PROJECT STATUS
CONCEPT

YEAR
2018

FIRM LOCATION
HANGZHOU
CHINA

Coral Seafood Restaurant
Kish, Iran
BNS Studio

TYPE
HOSPITALITY:
UNBUILT HOSPITALITY

WINNER
POPULAR CHOICE

PROJECT STATUS
CONCEPT

YEAR
2018

FIRM LOCATION
TEHRAN
IRAN

The Coral Seafood Restaurant sits on a breakwater that is 590 feet (180 meters) in length, located by the beautiful Kish Island in the Persian Gulf, adjacent to the Marina Park Hotel. This unique building looks as if it were afloat in the middle of the sea and includes spaces such as an indoor hall, an outdoor lounge, and an open-air coffee shop with lampshadelike umbrellas that provide shade during the day and illuminate the night. Like musical notes, the openings along the building's linear volume add rhythm and harmony to the design. These windows not only frame the view of the sea, but also create dynamic and pleasant spaces. In reference to the coral reef of Kish Island, abstract coral forms were used as a primary design concept.

Thailand Creative and Design Center
Bangkok, Thailand

Department of ARCHITECTURE Co.

TYPE
INSTITUTIONAL:
GOVERNMENT &
MUNICIPAL BUILDINGS

DETAILS — PLUS:
ARCHITECTURE + FURNITURE

WINNER
JURY
POPULAR CHOICE

PROJECT STATUS
BUILT

YEAR
2018

FIRM LOCATION
BANGKOK
THAILAND

Thailand Creative and Design Center (TCDC) is a government agency with a mission to inspire and propel the country's creative economy. It provides a broad range of resources and services: a design library, a material library, a coworking space, a maker space, exhibitions, lectures, workshops, and more.

Changing locations, TCDC has moved into a wing of the historical Grand Postal Building. A translucent furniture system was especially designed by the architect to represent the essence of what TCDC provides: inspiration and knowledge. The system is conceived to contain everything from books to magazines, material samples, digital media, mini exhibitions, brainstorm boards, announcements, and design products.

Within the framework, the furniture system varies for different functions, including bookshelves, exhibition pods, material sample display, info counter, and signage.

As such, the gridded translucent interior design is used as an architectural tool to organize spaces. Within the historical building, the new furniture system is inserted as an object, offset from the existing envelope and clearly revealing architectural features from the 1930s. The present-day material in its light, translucent, blurring, and glowing quality facilitates a dialogue with the grand character of the historical shell. At TCDC, the new and the old are interestingly contrasting with, enhancing, and complementing one another.

Palace of Justice
Córdoba, Spain

Mecanoo and Ayesa

The new Palace of Justice in Córdoba, Spain, is located in Arroyo del Moro, which is characteristically dominated by anonymous housing blocks.

Those blocks that define the urban fabric of the zone were not capable of generating appealing public space or offering something new to the city, even though collectively they form a compact and coherent urban identity. The addition of a public institution to the area creates the opportunity to upgrade the public realm and add a civic quality to the relatively new neighborhood.

The massing strategy creates urban integration through fragmentation. It follows a similar strategy to the spontaneous growth process of medieval cities, resulting in a volume that is carefully sculpted to adapt to

the surrounding context. From the main entrance, the interior organization is easily recognizable. A central spine creates a circulation axis that connects to the various programs of the building.

The internal functions become more private higher up in the building. At the level of the square, the courthouse features an open ground floor that contains the most public sections, such as courtrooms, the marriage registry, and a restaurant. High-security offices are situated off the upper courtyards, and the archives and jail cells are found below ground level.

TYPE
INSTITUTIONAL:
GOVERNMENT &
MUNICIPAL BUILDINGS

WINNER
POPULAR CHOICE

PROJECT STATUS
BUILT

YEAR
2017

FIRM LOCATIONS
DELFT
THE NETHERLANDS

CÓRDOBA
SPAIN

The Owsley Brown II History Center at the Filson Historical Society
Louisville, KY, USA

de Leon & Primmer
Architecture Workshop

TYPE
INSTITUTIONAL:
HIGHER EDUCATION &
RESEARCH FACILITIES

WINNER
JURY

PROJECT STATUS
BUILT

YEAR
2017

FIRM LOCATION
LOUISVILLE, KY
USA

Based in Louisville, Kentucky, the Filson Historical Society collects, curates, and archives the rich narrative of the Ohio River Valley region, offering an ambitious range of educational programs and cultural resources that support this focus. As one component of a comprehensive campus expansion that knits together historic structures and a new public plaza, the Owsley Brown II History Center is a thirty-thousand-square-foot facility (2,790 square meters) that provides multiuse event spaces, archival storage, and a digitization lab.

In a deliberate contrast to Filson's existing headquarters within the Ferguson Mansion, the project explores ways to reinforce a new presence for the organization as a welcoming and accessible public resource for the community and the region.

Employing a playful brick facade that emphasizes material layering made possible through modern construction methods, the new History Center provides a visually open structure that highlights its primary programmatic functions. Typically hidden areas—such as archival storage—are revealed and reinterpreted as opportunities to display Filson's cultural assets. Embedded throughout the building are transparent passageways and impromptu exhibition spaces that encourage exploration and discovery.

Informed by in-depth research and documentation of the area's development patterns dating back to the eighteenth century, the new facility is specifically rooted in its immediate context while being clearly of its time.

Faculty of Architecture and Environmental Design Kigali
Kigali, Rwanda

Patrick Schweitzer & Associés

TYPE
INSTITUTIONAL:
HIGHER EDUCATION &
RESEARCH FACILITIES

WINNER
POPULAR CHOICE

PROJECT STATUS
BUILT

YEAR
2017

FIRM LOCATION
STRASBOURG
FRANCE

The architecture practice Patrick Schweitzer & Associés responded to the international call launched by the government of Rwanda in March 2012 for the construction of the new Faculty of Architecture in Kigali. The school covers an area of 60,278 square feet (5,600 square meters) and has the capacity to accommodate six hundred students. It is located in the University of Rwanda's College of Science and Technology campus in the Nyarugenge district.

The building is the result of a global site analysis. Its architecture is inspired by the territory and by colors and shapes found in nature, and the four natural elements are represented in the conception of the building. Fire is seen in the orange color, water in the inner garden, air in the circulation, and earth in the lava rock and rammed earth.

The practice was determined to build a project that is in itself a pedagogic tool. And indeed, the architecture shows the building process to the students. It is fundamental for the aspiring young architects to be encouraged to use local resources. Creating an example, ceilings and joineries are made of local wood, slabs were cast in place, and traditional removable formwork was also used, all nurturing local sectors.

Infinity Kindergarten
Shanghai, China

Office Mass

On an irregularly shaped piece of land, encircled by a typical villa area in Shanghai, Office Mass tried to break through the dual restriction of the surrounding environment and norms through design strategies that create an ideal space for children in the city.

The architects were faced with the problem of how to respond to such a passive site with a positive attitude, especially as there was a decrease in land-use efficiency caused by irregular terrain.

Without interfering with the external conditions, the most positive gesture might be to create an ideal place, like a bonsai, which is clearly microscopic and partial, but contains our expectation and imagination.

Unlike with ordinary centralized kindergartens, the architects divided the building into houses, corridors, and courtyards. These spatial components, stacked like building blocks, loosely form the infinity symbol.

Classrooms are arranged in a cluster layout, while the other house—the one with a diagonally sloping roof—unifies the two classes on the first and second floor into one volume.

The corridor connects the scattered houses and accommodates the kindergarten's service spaces. The architects deliberately widened the circular corridor and integrated it with the outdoor space to make it a space where children can meet and play.

TYPE
INSTITUTIONAL:
KINDERGARTENS

WINNER
JURY

PROJECT STATUS
BUILT

YEAR
2017

FIRM LOCATION
SHANGHAI
CHINA

Wondrous Light
Children's House
Singapore

CHANG Architects

This is a children's place offering a living, breathing form of nurturing. It allows self-discovery of the individual, as well as understanding and being aware of oneself through the exploration of the senses, through physical movement, and through interacting with others and the environment.

The space is about making connections to the surroundings, to humanity, and to the cosmos, and all of life's experiences as these unfold through daily encounters. Designed with the children's scale, perspectives, and psychologies in mind, the crafted spaces offer a variety of spatial experiences that support emotional developments. Varying planar qualities through the use of natural and recycled plywood panels supply different experiences of touch and feel with changing texture, line works, and formal expressions.

This project does not aim to educate children through academics nor expose them to the latest digital technologies.

It offers a homely environment where children feel calm and are secure to enjoy free, self-directed play; to develop a sense of empathy. Through open-ended explorations and enhancements of their senses, they become emotionally stable, more authentic, imaginative, and conscious of their state of being.

TYPE
INSTITUTIONAL: KINDERGARTENS

WINNER
POPULAR CHOICE

PROJECT STATUS
BUILT

YEAR
2017

FIRM LOCATION
SINGAPORE

Tianjin Binhai Library
Binhai, China

MVRDV

MVRDV collaborated with the Tianjin Urban Planning and Design Institute (TUPDI) to realize the Tianjin Binhai Library. Celebrated and divisive at once, the 362,740-square-foot (33,700 square meters) cultural center features a luminous spherical auditorium around which floor-to-ceiling bookcases cascade. The undulating bookshelf is the building's main spatial device and is used to frame the space.

The library was commissioned by Tianjin Binhai Municipality and is located in the cultural center of Binhai district in Tianjin. The library, situated adjacent to a park, is one of a cluster of five cultural buildings designed by an international cadre of architects. All buildings are connected by a public corridor underneath a glass canopy designed by GMP.

The building's mass extrudes upward from the site and is punctured by a spherical auditorium in the center. Bookshelves are arrayed on either side of the sphere and act as everything from stairs to seating, even continuing along the ceiling to create an illuminated topography. These contours also continue along the two full glass facades that connect the library to the park on the outside and the public corridor on the inside, serving as louvers to protect the interior against excessive sunlight while luring visitors in.

TYPE
INSTITUTIONAL:
LIBRARIES

WINNER
JURY
POPULAR CHOICE

PROJECT STATUS
BUILT

YEAR
2017

FIRM LOCATION
ROTTERDAM
THE NETHERLANDS

Wall of Knowledge
El Jadida, Morocco
Tarik Zoubdi Architecte

The Wall of Knowledge is a middle school in the city of El Jadida, Morocco. The irregular shape of the site and its orientation to the sun suggested a spatial distribution of the project in three main areas: the central area is defined by a building reserved for teaching, which occupies the middle of the plot and serves as a landmark for the neighborhood; the northern area includes all sport facilities, and the southern area is kept vacant for further school extensions.

Walking distances are short, and the facade unfolds to a public plaza, which serves as a social space and a security perimeter. The hermetic and protective character of the facade is meant to evoke a monumental image. Covered with local stones, it is a tribute to the architecture of the old Portuguese city of El Jadida.

The metallic *mashrabiya* skin, adorned with the "universal alphabet" as a symbol of tolerance, protects the interior from the sun. The central lobby allows quick access to all major locations of the main building through passageways and over footbridges that form an architectural promenade around the central courtyard, like the patios of traditional Moroccan schools.

TYPE
INSTITUTIONAL:
PRIMARY & HIGH SCHOOLS

WINNER
JURY
POPULAR CHOICE

PROJECT STATUS
CONCEPT

YEAR
2017

FIRM LOCATION
CASABLANCA
MOROCCO

Hamedan Chamber of Commerce
Hamedan, Iran

United Design Architects

TYPE
INSTITUTIONAL:
UNBUILT INSTITUTIONAL

WINNER
JURY
POPULAR CHOICE

PROJECT STATUS
CONCEPT

YEAR
2018

FIRM LOCATION
PORTLAND, OR
USA

Persian art and architecture is grounded in abstract geometries and geometric patterns. As a design genesis, the architects understood that the formal, organizational, and aesthetic properties of a geometric pattern system would create a unifying language for a multiuse building with a complicated program and challenging access requirements. Therefore, in combining the precedent of cultural identity with the organizational properties of patterns, the development of a geometric pattern became the design basis of the Hamedan Chamber of Commerce.

Spatial organization, formal composition, and relational elements were adapted and synthesized through the pattern, which integrates site, design, and building functions into an associative whole. The associative pattern also fuses the heterogeneous program through dividing and distributing functions in the stacking of floors as well as horizontal zoning.

The geometry of the pattern allows for vertical and horizontal adaptation, while the weaving of the resulting strip morphologies generates a form. This system also translates into the geometric language of the facade and the incorporation of the greater landscape. In the program, the tri-axis configuration on the ground floor creates two principal VIP and general public entrances, with a third arc responding to the site's parameters and surrounding woodlands.

Farm to Table
Woodside, CA, USA

Arterra Landscape Architects

TYPE
LANDSCAPE & PLANNING:
LANDSCAPE DESIGN — PRIVATE

WINNER
JURY

PROJECT STATUS
BUILT

YEAR
2017

FIRM LOCATION
SAN FRANCISCO, CA
USA

An underlying geometric order organizes an array of outdoor rooms in a landscape entirely dedicated to food production and entertainment.

Raised beds, an orchard, and a chicken coop provide the harvest and natural ingredients for a client who has a strong culinary background. The outdoor kitchen, a pizza oven, and a large dining terrace offer places to cook and enjoy the process. Edible plants are scattered throughout the plan so the owners' children can learn about food

production firsthand. Naturally, they are able to discover herbs and fruits to snack on as they make their way around the property, from the pool to the bocce court to their daily visit of the roaming chickens. A variety of outdoor rooms and recreation areas radiate outward from a central courtyard, thereby providing a framework to experience the natural habitat around it.

On the Edge of the Continent
Jenner, CA, USA

Shades of Green Landscape Architecture

On a windswept grassy ridge high above the Pacific Ocean sits a pyramid-shaped house with awe-inspiring views of the surrounding hills rolling down to the sea. Although breathtaking, the site posed a significant challenge of designing usable spaces and effective circulation on a steep hillside.

On the hillside, the challenge was to create terraced, livable outdoor rooms, while retaining and celebrating the natural landform. Aligned with the grade, the terraces project minimally from the hillside and feel embraced by the natural meadow. On the upper terrace are located a bocce court and grassy seating area. Below is a vegetable garden with planters and steps made of weathering steel. At the lowest largest terrace is an infinity pool that blends earth with sky, and in turn causes the terrace to disappear when viewed from above.

In addition to the built elements, the project includes a drought tolerant plant palette that could handle poor soils and harsh coastal conditions. The plantings, which feature waving grasses, coastal perennials, and interesting succulents, visually connect the terraces and weave the design into the natural landscape.

TYPE
LANDSCAPE & PLANNING:
LANDSCAPE DESIGN — PRIVATE

WINNER
POPULAR CHOICE

PROJECT STATUS
BUILT

YEAR
2016

FIRM LOCATION
SAUSALITO, CA
USA

Eda U. Gerstacker Grove
Ann Arbor, MI, USA

Stoss Landscape Urbanism

TYPE
LANDSCAPE & PLANNING:
LANDSCAPE DESIGN — PUBLIC

WINNER
JURY

PROJECT STATUS
BUILT

YEAR
2016

FIRM LOCATION
BOSTON, MA
USA

The Eda U. Gerstacker Grove is a renovation of an underutilized campus quad at the heart of the University of Michigan's North Campus, home to the Schools of Engineering, Art, and Architecture.

Designed as a lush and active space, the grove can accommodate a range of rotating performances, events, and everyday activities. It starts as a flexible green quad, with clearings marked in an elegant grove. The central plaza can host larger-scale activities, like

musical and arts performances, and student and alumni events, and organizes casual play or recreation while conveying the many students on campus from class to class.

The namesake grove is designed to amplify daily and seasonal change, bringing to life different parts of the quad as warmer and cooler areas for gathering and hosting a series of changing installations by students. Infiltration gardens planted with bald cypress collect rainwater on-site,

while a weather station reads rainfall, temperature, and other data illuminated over one hundred acrylic rods with vibrant LEDs to create a sparkling dance of color and light.

The Block
Dubai, United Arab Emirates
desert INK

Open to the public since February 2018, the Block is already performing exceptionally well, with two large festivals held at the venue within its first month of opening alone.

During the seven-month construction period, over seven hundred surplus concrete blocks—left on the site by the Dubai Canal's developers—were stacked to create a multitude of possible features and playful items. Reusing the stacks determined the central design direction and defined the park's aesthetic, but ultimately prevented over 22,000 tons (twenty thousand metric tonnes) of concrete from going to a landfill.

The park features an outdoor gym, multisports court, urban beach, skate park and open lawns. At the center of the park, the blocks are arranged to create an intriguing labyrinth-like ravine that is naturally shaded, the floor of which is finished with recycled rubber and walls adorned with climbing holds.

The landscape architecture firm, desert INK, ensured that construction materials are reusable, recycled, and locally sourced. The locally produced concrete paving can be lifted for reuse upon decommissioning, while the entire warehouse structure is designed to be reassembled at a future site. The blocks themselves are reusable, while timber decks utilize former scaffolding planks rather than virgin, imported materials.

TYPE
LANDSCAPE & PLANNING:
LANDSCAPE DESIGN — PUBLIC

WINNER
POPULAR CHOICE

PROJECT STATUS
BUILT

YEAR
2018

FIRM LOCATION
DUBAI
UNITED ARAB EMIRATES

11th Street Bridge Park

OMA and OLIN

The 11th Street Bridge Park is a place of exchange, a new civic space uniting two historically separated communities and supporting environmental, economic, cultural, and physical health. Originally commissioned through a national design competition, the project, now in progress, will contribute to the civic fabric of Washington, D.C., through a multifunctional landscape, which promotes the health of the Anacostia River and its adjacent communities, acting as a model both nationally and globally.

The design began with a series of decommissioned bridge piers, left in place in the Anacostia River when a highway bridge was demolished and relocated. Building on top of this existing infrastructure, the bridge park is composed of a series of rooms and active zones, including two sloped ramps that elevate visitors to maximized look-out points for viewing landmarks in either direction.

Each ramp terminates in a waterfall that visually connects the ramps to the river below. In addition to demonstrating how plants cleanse captured rainwater, the waterfalls above the bridge deck provide a cooling breeze and calming sounds. To encourage visitors to the bridge and neighboring communities, the design includes amenities for comfort and refreshment and an open plaza for markets, festivals, and theatrical performances.

TYPE
LANDSCAPE & PLANNING:
UNBUILT MASTERPLAN

WINNER
JURY

PROJECT STATUS
CONCEPT

YEAR
2018

FIRM LOCATIONS
NEW YORK, NY
USA

PHILADELPHIA, PA
USA

LANDSCAPE & PLANNING:
UNBUILT MASTERPLAN

Cuchi Organic Eco Farm
Cuchi, Vietnam

IF (Integrated Field)

Since the Vietnam War ended, Vietnam joined the global capitalism caravan. The ensuing dramatic urbanization and economic growth strained the food industry.

Cuchi Organic Eco Farm is a design proposal for a 1,500-acre (six hundred hectares) decommissioned rubber plantation in Cuchi, Vietnam. The client acquired the land and aimed to transform the underutilized site into an organic food production farm providing animal feed, livestock, fruit, and vegetation in a closed-cycle operation.

Users experience the organic food cycle through a journey on the farm. The relationship between animal and plant is boldly emphasized in visitor routes and activities offered. Different farming zones are defined as learning nodes, such as the Agroforestry node, Food Cycle node, and Livestock node. The visitor route is designed to pass each node as a learning spot, concluding in the main area. These learning nodes are key to understanding how the organic process works in reality, offering visitors the experience of and empirical

knowledge in food production. Eventually, understanding leads to trust in the farm, to trust in food.

The project also offers farm-stay accommodation, a farm-to-table restaurant, a farmers market, and a cofarming area where indiviuals can rent plots to farm. The existing rubber tree vegetation has been selectively kept as a windbreaker for air contamination.

TYPE
LANDSCAPE & PLANNING:
UNBUILT MASTERPLAN

WINNER
POPULAR CHOICE

PROJECT STATUS
CONCEPT

YEAR
2018

FIRM LOCATION
BANGKOK
THAILAND

Cleveland Rooftop
Sydney, Australia

SJB Architects

TYPE
RESIDENTIAL:
APARTMENT

WINNER
JURY

PROJECT STATUS
BUILT

YEAR
2016

FIRM LOCATION
SURRY HILLS
AUSTRALIA

Perched atop an adaptively reused industrial building, this new rooftop structure provides a welcoming retreat for its inhabitants—a place fulfilling the function of a true home within the dense city.

Internally, the building is organized around its connections to the outside. Skylights punctuate the roof form to deliver light, while a deep cut in the living space brings the landscape into the home. Private spaces, including bathrooms and sleeping quarters, are formally arranged to enable a "full house" while protecting privacy.

While not attempting to directly reference the aesthetic of the original building below, the penthouse addition aims to follow its lead, delivering a raw concrete space with large expanses of glass to encourage light penetration. The material palette is simple, raw, and not intended to be overly detailed. The use of concrete throughout, timber floors, and granite paving both inside and outside the dwelling delivers a home with a relaxed feel.

The garden's flora is predominantly native, creating an oasis for indigenous birds and insects. This small piece of sky landscape aims to contribute to the opportunistic network of small inner city native landscape spaces and public parks that provide respite for fauna.

Ibirapuera Apartment
São Paulo, Brazil

FCstudio

The Ibirapuera Apartment project, located in São Paulo, Brazil, is designed with two main priorities in mind. Firstly, it allows views onto the nearby Ibirapuera urban park designed by Oscar Niemeyer, and secondly, it promotes strong spatial integration between the different areas of the apartment. The entire space contains furniture chosen or developed by the architect, in order to create a coherently radiant atmosphere in each environment; details in chromatic appearance, dimension, and essence have been carefully considered. A horizontal shelf identifies the TV room and seems to stretch the space. The lunch room is separated by a wine rack that can be used for serving in the dining room. On the balcony, a singular wood-and-stone table promotes the social integration requested by the client for this area.

A circular bench and the Volpi panel are pieces created specifically for this project. The bench is held together by two transversal inclined steel plates that unite the five wooden panels without letting them touch each other. The natural aging process will heighten the value by further accentuating the specific properties of the materials. The Volpi panel is composed of wooden triangles aligned on the front of the piece, thereby creating a light-and-shadows experience and, at the same time, gently separating two spaces without closing them off completely. The special piece is in dialogue with the surrounding designs and was named after the artist Alfredo Volpi Claira Machado.

TYPE
RESIDENTIAL:
APARTMENT

WINNER
POPULAR CHOICE

PROJECT STATUS
CONCEPT

YEAR
2015

FIRM LOCATION
SÃO PAULO
BRAZIL

Canaletto
London, UK
UNStudio

TYPE
RESIDENTIAL:
MULTIUNIT HOUSING —
HIGH-RISE (16+ FLOORS)

WINNER
JURY

PROJECT STATUS
BUILT

YEAR
2017

FIRM LOCATION
AMSTERDAM
THE NETHERLANDS

Offering waterside living, the 237,000-square-foot (twenty-two thousand square meters) and thirty-one-story Canaletto residential tower in London comprises studios, one-and two-bedroom apartments, a variety of three bedrooms, and one distinct penthouse with a full rooftop. Canaletto also includes shared amenities, such as a swimming pool, health club, media room, and resident's club lounge with a terrace on the twenty-fourth floor.

UNStudio's design for the tower, which is located in the London borough of Islington, incorporates the remodeling of the facade, a streamlining of the building's mass, and a contrasting of scale and detail atypical of a residential tower.

The materialization of the facade draws from examples of detailing and the contrasting of materials that is readily expressed in product or furniture design. The modeling of the balconies within each grouped cluster lends variability to the facade and the living experience for the residents in the building.

The project additionally offers sustainability benefits. The surface modeling creates opportunities for shading, balancing good internal daylight and views with reduced heat gains. The articulation of the facade will additionally reduce wind down drafts and, in combination with the canopy at the base of the building, provide an improved pedestrian microclimate.

Jersey City Urby
Jersey City, NJ, USA

Concrete

Jersey City Urby is the second Urby that is realized: a new rental housing concept in the Greater New York area built from the ground up with the needs of contemporary urban citizens in mind. Jersey City Urby consists of 762 rental apartments in a sixty-nine-story tower—with two more towers planned—and is located right on the Hudson River in the heart of Jersey City, a five-minute subway ride away from New York's World Trade Center. The tower shapes the new Jersey City skyline and is the tallest building with stunning views of downtown Manhattan.

The architectural design of Jersey City Urby reflects the playful and organic nature of the Urby brand. The tower is made up of stacked blocks, creating a vertical neighborhood that focuses on openness, space, and connection. The projected blocks result in an expressive and progressive architecture—like Urby itself—and at the same time create a larger diversity in unit types to serve a broader clientele. The windows are straightforward in their design celebrating daylight and views. The crown of the building is illuminated at night with an intensity that differs to reflect the activity in the building: the more people are at home, the brighter the light shines into the night.

TYPE
RESIDENTIAL:
MULTIUNIT HOUSING —
HIGH-RISE (16+ FLOORS)

WINNER
POPULAR CHOICE

PROJECT STATUS
BUILT

YEAR
2017

FIRM LOCATION
AMSTERDAM
THE NETHERLANDS

Cirqua Apartments
Melbourne, Australia

BKK Architects

The Cirqua Apartments project represents a shift in Melbourne's multiresidential market that has been evolving over the past four years. Prospective owners are increasingly buying into the apartment market (over detached housing) as a matter of choice rather than necessity. Whereas previously apartments were largely aimed at the investment market or those who could not afford to buy a house, the majority of Cirqua's tenants comprise owner-occupiers. This shift is typified in the design approach of Cirqua, which offers larger apartments, greater diversity of type (thirty-eight out of forty-two apartments are unique), spacious balconies, and generous landscaping.

Situated on a steeply sloping site, the project involved the consolidation of two neighboring properties into a single block. The design has been carried out to provide a strong sense of address for tenants while maintaining a street rhythm and scale that stitches the project into its local context.

Cirqua is designed to carefully consider accessibility and passive environmental performance, with all the apartments' bedrooms and living areas having direct access to natural light and ventilation. Generous glazing in circular shape maximizes connections to the surrounding garden by offering wide views on the significant landscaping integrated into the design.

TYPE
RESIDENTIAL:
MULTIUNIT HOUSING —
LOW-RISE (1–4 FLOORS)

WINNER
JURY
POPULAR CHOICE

PROJECT STATUS
BUILT

YEAR
2017

FIRM LOCATION
MELBOURNE
AUSTRALIA

Light House
Zhubei City, Taiwan

Shen Ting Tseng
Architects

TYPE
RESIDENTIAL:
MULTIUNIT HOUSING —
MID-RISE (5–15 FLOORS)

WINNER
JURY
POPULAR CHOICE

PROJECT STATUS
BUILT

YEAR
2017

FIRM LOCATION
TAIPEI
TAIWAN

Light-House is located in Hsinchu County, Taiwan. This multistory residential building block is designed under close consideration of common Taiwanese terrace-style houses.

The project proposes another version of a contemporary housing model for Taiwan, encouraging spatial encounters in connection with the natural environment by introducing the elements of "breathing pockets" between spaces and within each level—courtyards, balconies, terraces, and light wells. These elements are designed in relationship to the internal staircases, rooms, and open spaces in order to generate a layered spatial relationship (vertically and horizontally) within each multilevel unit. This layered interior layout creates private spaces within open spaces, therefore generating a sense of retreat within a vast space.

Natural light and wind flow through the interiors through layers of square openings and windows on the southern elevation, transforming the internal spaces with varying lighting conditions throughout the day. Natural light extends to every corner of the home, creating brighter interior spaces, which allow for increased growth and vitality of domestic greenery. Externally, instead of a continuous facade treatment, the facade recedes inward in order to construct a visual gap between the houses while retaining spatial possibilities for chance encounters between neighboring properties and occupants.

Ring House
Agia Galini, Greece
decaARCHITECTURE

TYPE
RESIDENTIAL:
PRIVATE HOUSE
(L 3,000–5,000 SQ. FT.)

WINNER
JURY

PROJECT STATUS
BUILT

YEAR
2016

FIRM LOCATION
ATHENS
GREECE

The Ring House is located on the southern coast of Crete, only 165 nautical miles from the Sahara desert. Two concrete beams follow the topography of the hill to define the outline of the house. The ring is articulated by these concrete beams. It provides shaded areas, well-ventilated interiors, and surfaces for solar collection panels, and protects an inner garden planted with varieties of citrus trees and edible plants. Altogether, the house and its garden are designed to form a temperate microclimate—an oasis within an intensely beautiful but physically demanding environment.

At a broader scale, the house is a landscape preservation effort. In the past, the topography has been severely scarred by the random and informal carving of roads. The excavation material extracted during the house's construction was used to recover the original morphology of the land. Furthermore, a thorough survey of the native flora was conducted in order to understand the predominant biotopes in the different slopes of the plot. During the spring preceding construction, seeds were collected on-site and cultivated in a greenhouse to grow more seeds. These were later sowed over the road scars for the native regeneration of the flora.

Carrara House
Lagos, Portugal

Mario Martins Atelier

TYPE
RESIDENTIAL:
PRIVATE HOUSE
(L 3,000–5,000 SQ. FT.)

WINNER
POPULAR CHOICE

PROJECT STATUS
BUILT

YEAR
2017

FIRM LOCATION
LAGOS
PORTUGAL

Carrara House has a certain sculptural character—curved and dynamic forms have been treated like a volume sculpted from a rough block that has been brought to life. At Carrara House, more angular and longer forms are sculpted in a parallelepiped shape where full and empty spaces coexist as organic areas. Special attention is to be paid to the terrace, which functions as an embellishment or a pinnacle. Its deliberately dry and simple language demonstrates clarity and a sense for proportion.

As an integral part of the house, the terrace provides a frame for a privileged place, giving shade and establishing a physical relationship to the rooms looking out to sea. The suspended pool is part of this sculpted volume, intensely white, interspersed with the authenticity of marble's irregular patterns, which appear to show the way to the entrance and other areas of access. The project consists of weight and lightness, throughout all of which the interior and exterior meet in pleasant corners, sheltered or deliberately exposed, to enjoy this place and the horizon distant, but as simple and linear as the design of this house.

Square House
Stone Ridge, NY, USA
LEVENBETTS

TYPE
RESIDENTIAL:
PRIVATE HOUSE
(M 1,000–3,000 SQ. FT.)

WINNER
JURY

PROJECT STATUS
BUILT

YEAR
2017

FIRM LOCATION
NEW YORK, NY
USA

The Square House is designed around a very simple concept: architecture can completely engage landscape not just through its apertures but also from its organizational basis and its approach to what it means to be inside and outside.

There is no front door or back door or formal entry. The house is conceived as a series of rooms that can be accessed directly from outside, creating a fluid relationship between interior and exterior. The house also has no windows, only doors. The square plan

reinforces a nonhierarchical informal organization while still allowing each face of the building to offer a different experience of the landscape and light.

The material approach maximizes the sculptural and textural opportunities of cast concrete, allowing the building to sit in the landscape. The material challenges the house type and its domestic program by acting as both a massive threshold and a permeable surface through which domestic space and nature can comingle. Square

House is heated with the large fireplace and hot-water radiant heating cast into the concrete slab. Unsurprisingly, the house utilizes the thermal mass of the south-shaded concrete and uses very little energy.

Brick Cave
Hanoi, Vietnam

H&P Architects

The house is located in a suburban commune of Hanoi, Vietnam, which has undergone a rapid process of urbanization. The proposed structure of the house resembles that of a cave. Overall, it is made up of and enclosed by two layers of brick wall meeting one another at an intersection, with alternate green arrangements of vegetables and other plants.

Bricks have long been a familiar local material and are widely used in rural areas of Vietnam in combination with simple manual construction methods. The two built-in wall layers function as a filter to eliminate the adverse aspects of the external environment, namely sunshine, dust, and noise. Above, the outer wall is tilted inward in different diagonals to create better viewing angles onto the general landscape of the area. At the same time, this helps users in various locations inside the house to sense time and weather through the movement of shadows and air.

Brick Cave encompasses a chain of spaces interconnected through random apertures, gradually shifting from open/public to closed/private. The combination of openness and privacy creates diverse relationships with the surroundings and helps blur the boundaries between in and out, house and street, human and nature.

TYPE
RESIDENTIAL:
PRIVATE HOUSE
(M 1,000–3,000 SQ. FT.)

DETAILS — PLUS:
ARCHITECTURE + BRICK

WINNER
JURY
POPULAR CHOICE

PROJECT STATUS
BUILT

YEAR
2017

FIRM LOCATION
HANOI
VIETNAM

Grove House
Bridgehampton, NY, USA

Roger Ferris + Partners

This private residence located in the Hamptons was designed as an immersive yet modern and natural retreat. Situated along a natural ravine and protected wetlands, the residence consists of three simple gable-shaped volumes that create a dialogue between the natural grasslands and the built environment.

The architects' objective was to create a single-family residence with a shared living area, private bedrooms, and an art studio while taking advantage of the lush landscape that surrounds the site. Two of the volumes, delicately connected by a glass breezeway, house the public and private living spaces of the home. A third volume stands alone, providing space for the artist studio on the second floor.

A contemporary interpretation of a common New England building form, each volume is shrouded in horizontal wood slats, which seamlessly wrap all wall and roof surfaces. Planes of glass provide both a visual and physical connection to the natural surrounding landscape. A public great room is centrally located, acting as a social hub for family and guest interaction. Within the great room, special attention was paid to the design of the architectural concrete fireplace, countertops, and black steel sash windows.

TYPE
RESIDENTIAL:
PRIVATE HOUSE
(XL >5,000 SQ. FT.)

WINNER
JURY

PROJECT STATUS
BUILT

YEAR
2017

FIRM LOCATION
WESTPORT, CT
USA

Casa Península
São Paulo, Brazil

Bernardes Arquitetura

Casa Península, a weekend home in a coastal city close to São Paulo, Brazil, is composed of three stacked abstract volumes that have been delicately positioned on a steep slope overlooking the Atlantic Ocean for minimum topographic impact. The house is divided into three parts: the rectangular base and the triangular superior volume, which contain more private areas; and the transparent space inbetween them where the common areas are located.

The suspended triangular volume creates shaded balconies protected from direct sunlight, while the more enclosed and monolithic base provides intimate spaces. The tension between the two architectural programs creates negative, translucent spaces that visually connect with the ever-present landscape.

TYPE
RESIDENTIAL:
PRIVATE HOUSE
(XL >5,000 SQ. FT.)

WINNER
POPULAR CHOICE

PROJECT STATUS
BUILT

YEAR
2017

FIRM LOCATION
RIO DE JANEIRO
BRAZIL

Mylla Cabin
Jevnaker, Norway

Mork Ulnes Architects

Mylla is a small cabin located in a towering pine forest outside of Oslo. Designed as a retreat for a geologist and his family, the building sits firmly on a hilltop and is shaped by the forces of the landscape around it. Though planning regulations required a gable roof, Mylla splits the gable in half to create four shed roofs that radiate in a pinwheel configuration. Two sheltered outdoor spaces are created, which are protected from the wind and from snow shed; the exterior is clad simply with untreated heart pine planks, which register the seasons as they gray and weather with time.

The compact interior, finished in plywood and unified with a continuous roof canopy, can house up to ten people across three dedicated bedrooms and two full bathrooms. Custom plywood furniture—including bed frames, bunk beds, a couch, a dining table, benches, and shelves— is found throughout. The wings of the house engage four distinct characters of the landscape by framing them neatly: the great room looks onto Mylla Lake, the guest room looks toward the rolling hillside, the kids' room looks up at the sky, and the bedroom has a private view of the towering forest beyond.

TYPE
RESIDENTIAL:
PRIVATE HOUSE
(XS <1,000 SQ. FT.)

WINNER
JURY

PROJECT STATUS
BUILT

YEAR
2017

FIRM LOCATION
SAN FRANCISCO, CA
USA

Iturbide Studio
Coyoacán, Mexico

Taller Mauricio Rocha + Gabriela Carrillo

This project is in the Niño Jesus neighborhood, just a few steps from Graciela Iturbide's home. In this context rises a small tower of just three levels that literally extrudes its floor plan to become a solid piece of clay, deconstructed to its own materiality in very fine and almost imperceptible tensions of steel.

On the interior, three planes of wood, concrete, and marble appear tensed from one side to another, creating a pair of voids of multiple heights, which in the near future will become patios with gardens. The interior facades insinuate almost imperceptibly the conditions of the context.

The services, circulation, and a long bookshelf group as a vertical element that integrates into the walls to practically disappear and highlight the clay volume.

Most importantly, the project seeks silence, synthesis, continuity, and a repetitive, almost obsessive use of a singular material. It aspires to become mass and emptiness, an ethereal volume that disappears with the light and shadow.

TYPE
RESIDENTIAL:
PRIVATE HOUSE
(XS <1,000 SQ. FT.)

WINNER
POPULAR CHOICE

PROJECT STATUS
BUILT

YEAR
2016

FIRM LOCATION
MEXICO CITY
MEXICO

A Room with a View
Toronto, ON, Canada
Superkul

TYPE
RESIDENTIAL:
RESIDENTIAL INTERIORS

WINNER
JURY

PROJECT STATUS
BUILT

YEAR
2017

FIRM LOCATION
TORONTO, ON
CANADA

This transformative intervention in a home in midtown Toronto comprises a complete renovation and addition to the second and third floors, thereby reorganizing and rearticulating the private spaces to meet a young family's evolving needs.

The suite is a refuge, a place of quiet serenity away from the demands of busy careers and frenetic urban life. The strategy to promote an enhanced connection to nature and the direct landscape includes a large south-facing window stretching from floor to ceiling and from wall to wall.

White oak dominates: its warmth and pleasing grain registers in the floors, walls, ceiling, and millwork. To create a contrast, black steel is utilized as a framing element and matte-black light fixtures adorn walls and ceilings. Above the bathtub, the skylight emerges as the room's focal point and provides an additional source of daylight while further allowing a connection to the sky and surrounding trees. Materially consistent with the walls, ceiling, and floor, the oak-sheathed planar facets create an intriguingly sculptural void that channels light into the space and invites constantly shifting patterns of sun and shadow throughout the day.

Malangen
Malangen, Norway

Stinessen Arkitektur

TYPE
RESIDENTIAL:
RESIDENTIAL INTERIORS

WINNER
POPULAR CHOICE

PROJECT STATUS
BUILT

YEAR
2017

FIRM LOCATION
TROMSØ
NORWAY

For a family with small children, the conceptual layout was conceived as several individual volumes connected via in-between spaces and a central winter garden, placed on a natural shelf in the terrain. The organization provides both privacy and room for several activities at the same time. It also reduces energy needed for heating in the cold climate, as various rooms and activities require different temperatures.

The central winter garden, with fireplace and outdoor kitchen, functions as the entrance to the building. From here the retreat opens up to the natural clearing in the forest, where one enters into either the main building or the annex.

Each group of rooms is placed in a separate volume not only to achieve an additional layer of privacy, but also to enhance the room's contact to the forest's clearing and the general outdoors in the transition spaces. A few steps lead down to the open-plan kitchen and living room, which are set low in the terrain and overlook the fjord and the afternoon sun to the west. A dedicated exit from the kitchen leads to the south-facing outdoor area, where the family can enjoy dinners on warm summer days.

Zaferanieh Residential Tower
Tehran, Iran

Challenge Studio
(Mohsen Tajeddin + Ehsan Karimi)

The site for the Zaferanieh Residential tower is located north of the city of Tehran, Iran. It is situated among the green orchards of the Alburz mountains, on one of the highest urban altitudes, offering a comprehensive view of the city. The primary design tenet was to reflect a level of luxury that is representative of the affluent residents as well as the high property value.

The design objective was to create an integrative relationship between structure and context, and to optimize the site's particular assets, including expansive views and green spaces. The residential units follow a modular design in such a way that each unit is made of a tri-axis module, which generates the global form through varying Tetris-like orientations and 180-degree rotations. The local modular form and associations create dynamic in-between spaces that draw the external surroundings inside the boundary of the built form, resulting in an interlacing of open and closed spaces. Consequently, by shifting the modular axes, each unit also includes diverse covered terraces with varying views and amenities—such as private swimming pools—while incorporating vertical gardens throughout the building.

TYPE
RESIDENTIAL:
UNBUILT — MULTIUNIT
HOUSING (L >10 FLOORS)

WINNER
JURY
POPULAR CHOICE

PROJECT STATUS
CONCEPT

YEAR
2018

FIRM LOCATION
EUGENE, OR
USA

Nolita Park Senior Residence
New York, NY, USA
THINK Architecture and Design

Consistent with its mandate to create affordable housing in New York, the city, through the Department of Housing Preservation and Development, identified this city-owned site in the Nolita neighborhood of Manhattan for affordable senior housing. This through-block site, running between Mott and Elizabeth Streets, is currently open and used by the community as a passive park. In recognition of the open space's importance to the community, the design brief for the development called for the retaining of five thousand square feet (465 square meters) of open space on the site for public use. The design was predicated on not just maximizing the public open space, but also making it visible and inviting from the streets.

To achieve this transparency, the masses of the two buildings were lifted up to the level of the second floor, and the necessary entry and retail space were developed as freestanding glass pavilions evolving around and through to the central garden—developed in collaboration with landscape architecture firm !melk—of the site. The project is composed of a mix of 116 one-bedroom and studio apartments with a residential area of 67,000 square feet (6,225 square meters).

TYPE
RESIDENTIAL:
UNBUILT — MULTIUNIT
HOUSING (S <10 FLOORS)

WINNER
JURY

PROJECT STATUS
CONCEPT

YEAR
2018

FIRM LOCATION
BROOKLYN, NY
USA

Sendo
Tijuana, Mexico

Estudio Santander

Tijuana has always been considered a city without definitions, a hybrid laboratory; it is neither defined as Mexican nor American. The recent real estate boom—fueled by high costs of living and high real estate prices in the neighboring San Diego—attracted developers from Mexico and abroad. However, most new projects are buildings that enclose themselves into vertical suburbs, effectively segregating and polarizing the social and urban fabric, thereby eroding the rich street life the city has to offer. Security is another important parameter that always had an impact in the morphology of residential housing, not only in Tijuana but throughout Mexico. As a result,

self-contained lifestyle compounds are dotting the city, providing relative safety and effectively withering street life. The rest of the city appears as a low-density horizontal sprawl: the segregated and polarized metropolis.

What strategies may be carried out to design buildings that offer security while engaging with the rest of the metropolis at the same time? Estudio Santander informed their proposal with traits of the *vecindad* typology: a mid-density housing model that successfully creates strong social fabrics and narratives.

TYPE
RESIDENTIAL:
UNBUILT — MULTIUNIT
HOUSING (S <10 FLOORS)

WINNER
POPULAR CHOICE

PROJECT STATUS
CONCEPT

YEAR
2018

FIRM LOCATION
BONITA, CA
USA

TYPE
RESIDENTIAL:
UNBUILT — PRIVATE HOUSE
(L >3,000 SQ. FT.)

WINNER
JURY

PROJECT STATUS
CONCEPT

YEAR
2018

FIRM LOCATION
AUCKLAND
NEW ZEALAND

X House
Queenstown, New Zealand

Monk Mackenzie Architects

Set in the foothills of the Remarkables mountain range in Queenstown, New Zealand, this private residence engages an uncompromising and breathtakingly beautiful landscape with an equally uncompromising architecture. Resolutely grounded in its site, the structure is anchored at four points but arches to bridge a natural watercourse bisecting the site.

To the east, the mountains present an imposing backdrop. To the west, the site descends to the lake edge, offering long views of sheer cliffs meeting the waterline. Here, the climate and weather are highly variable.

This landscape is all-encompassing. In this context, the architecture shapes a series of interior and exterior

spaces responding to particular and contrasting experiences, views, and climatic conditions. The building form strongly establishes and delineates the various opportunities for enclosure and inhabitation both internally and around its built perimeter. Interior spaces are created through a lifting up of the natural ground plane, revealing sites for various experiences of the landscape—sitting in the spa looking at the snow-covered mountains, hovering above the watercourse viewing the lake, embedding oneself within the ground.

Round Retreat

UNITEDLAB Associates

TYPE
RESIDENTIAL:
UNBUILT — PRIVATE HOUSE
(L >3,000 SQ. FT.)

WINNER
POPULAR CHOICE

PROJECT STATUS
CONCEPT

YEAR
2018

FIRM LOCATION
LONG ISLAND CITY, NY
USA

The building is anchored to the site by its relationship to natural elements. Four trees and a pond present a natural matrix from which the design arises. The formal strategy begins by encircling one existing tree and allowing the other trees to erode the perimeter, forming concave spaces in the doughnut-shaped form. In this way, trees and architecture form a figure-ground relationship. To reinforce the effect of a pure geometry, the "doughnut" is populated by circular spaces that are excavated from the whole, while creating free-flowing circulation spaces around the programmed areas. By liberating the structure of right angles, the design allows visitors to sync with the rhythms and orders of nature, as the architecture merges with its surroundings and becomes a serene backdrop for relaxation and healing. Unexpected glimpses of nature reveal themselves as occupants circumnavigate the building.

Each program element is distributed in cylindrical spaces, sized relative to its function. The relatively low occupancy for both the residence and the therapy uses allows for generous circulation spaces throughout the project. The sculptural passages, combined with the more intimate programmed areas, provide a warm atmosphere for groups to gather but also allow for quiet introspection and solitude when needed.

Pioneertown House
Pioneertown, CA, USA

PARA Project

TYPE
RESIDENTIAL:
UNBUILT — PRIVATE HOUSE
(S <3,000 SQ. FT.)

WINNER
JURY

PROJECT STATUS
CONCEPT

YEAR
2018

FIRM LOCATION
BROOKLYN, NY
USA

Pioneertown, California, was originally built in the 1940s as a live-in motion-picture set for actors. The seemingly alien Mojave landscape makes for a foreign counterpart to LA's urban culture. The particular site for this house is a five-acre (two hectares) boulder parcel owned by a West Hollywood art-dealer couple who wanted a weekend escape with an artist studio. There is an existing "homestead" masonry cabin on the property built in the 1950s. The design is a house developed around this house. Its organization takes cues from the landscape, but rather than using piles of boulders (objects), it experiments with piles of rooms (voids). It plays with a "pilgrimage" for these domestic types: rooms, courts, closets, counters, bookcases, and beds. These types all pile and gather around the homestead. The separation and movement between them is common ground with the landscape.

The most private space abuts a big boulder formation. A large U-shaped forecourt opens to the sky and separates the carport from the residence. Both the forecourt and the original homestead emphasize a vertical relationship with the site. The living areas, bedroom, and kitchen maintain quasi-cardinal horizontal relations. Some doubles emerge among favorite parts.

A House for Living

Hes.architects

For this project the architects were commissioned to design a house for a family that is in love with nature and greenery. The restrictions on the project included the narrow piece of land, which was blind from the east and west, and a height maximum of twenty-six feet (eight meters) from the ground.

The design divides the volume into closed private space and open public space on different levels. Further, to allocate natural light and ventilation throughout the space, the mass was divided. The space also includes a skylight on the lower level.

TYPE
RESIDENTIAL:
UNBUILT — PRIVATE HOUSE
(S <3,000 SQ. FT.)

WINNER
POPULAR CHOICE

PROJECT STATUS
CONCEPT

YEAR
2018

FIRM LOCATION
BENALMADENA
SPAIN

Vestre Fjord Park
Aalborg, Denmark
ADEPT

TYPE
SPORT & RECREATION:
RECREATION CENTERS

WINNER
JURY

PROJECT STATUS
BUILT

YEAR
2017

FIRM LOCATION
COPENHAGEN
DENMARK

Vestre Fjord Park is both a building and a natural landscape with a simple architectural design that contributes to the full experience of this unique site. Here, one finds a rich natural habitat offering varied outdoor activities.

It is the synergy between landscape, water spaces, and the users that gives Vestre Fjord Park its character. The ambition is to encourage contact with the fjord by allowing access to land and sea, while at the same time framing activities on the water with a multifunctional structure.

The park subdivides into smaller areas. The isthmus to the north—a narrow piece of land that connects two larger areas across an expanse of water— has facilities for sports associations and features unspoiled nature along

the fjord; the beach embraces the open-air swimming area with sand, water, and springboard diving; the woods and the wetlands to the west and south display dense vegetation in contrast to the open areas of the wedge and plains to the east.

The building acts as an integrated part of the promenade, with all paths clearly leading toward it. Bound together by the roofscape, small individual buildings provide space for a large variety of functions, including club facilities, a sauna, a café, changing rooms, and washrooms.

Bamboo Sports Hall
Chiang Mai, Thailand
Chiangmai Life Architects

Chiangmai Life Architects' Bamboo Sports Hall for Panyaden International School combines modern organic design, twenty-first-century engineering, and environmental sustainability.

The design was based on the lotus flower, which embodies the Buddhist teachings that are at the heart of the school's vision. The hall covers an area of 8,420 square feet (782 square meters) and hosts futsal, basketball, volleyball, and badminton courts, as well as a stage that can be lifted automatically.

In terms of function, the Bamboo Sports Hall stands out. The hall has a triple-layered roof with flowing organic curves that create natural ventilation and optimize natural light to brighten the interior without excessive heating.

The building also utilizes bamboo as a structural material with a pioneering ingenuity. The hall's newly developed bamboo trusses, with a span of over fifty-six feet (seventeen meters), were precisely calculated according to modern safety standards to withstand storms and earthquakes. Thus, they

have become reproducible elements that will help the credibility of bamboo as an alternative to steel.

A proud achievement is the Bamboo Sports Hall's zero-carbon footprint. The bamboo that was used absorbed more carbon than the amount of carbon that was emitted during treatment, transport, and construction.

TYPE
SPORT & RECREATION: RECREATION CENTERS

CONCEPTS — PLUS: ARCHITECTURE + ENGINEERING

WINNER
JURY
POPULAR CHOICE

PROJECT STATUS
CONCEPT

YEAR
2017

FIRM LOCATION
CHIANG MAI
THAILAND

Arena du Pays d'Aix
Aix-en-Provence, France

Auer Weber and
Christophe Gulizzi
Architecte

This newly built handball arena is situated on a freeway intersection in Aix-en-Provence. The facade is made up of metallic ellipses, stacked on top of each other like futuristic, layered contours. At first sight, the arena has no front or back, since every side of the facade is treated equally. Only very subtly do the differently arranged ellipses indicate the arena's front.

The sizable form embraces an events hall for eight thousand spectators; another smaller hall grants access to two thousand spectators. The arena reacts to the site through geometrical modifications: the ellipses, hovering above one another, and arranged with a much stronger shift toward the forecourt than to the other sides, form a large canopy to warmly welcome the arena's visitors. The undersides of the protruding ellipses are illuminated to show the building as a whole. In the evening, those lights additionally help to center the focus of the structure toward its forecourt.

TYPE
SPORT & RECREATION:
STADIUM / ARENA

WINNER
JURY

PROJECT STATUS
BUILT

YEAR
2017

FIRM LOCATIONS
MUNICH
GERMANY

AIX-EN-PROVENCE
FRANCE

Rwanda Cricket Stadium
Kigali, Rwanda

Light Earth Designs

The Rwanda Cricket Stadium by Light Earth Designs is formed of three linked parabolic vaults, closely mimicking the path of a bouncing ball while evoking the cherished hilly topography of Rwanda. The project empowers the development of the Rwandan economy using local labor-intensive construction materials and techniques.

The building evolves from the cut soil banking with vaults, adapted from the ancient Mediterranean technique of thin-tile vaulting for new environments, using compressed soil-cement tiles made from site-excavated earth. Local builders learned to implement this technique in East Africa for the first time. Through research developed by Michael Ramage at the University of Cambridge's Centre for Natural Material Innovation, geogrid reinforcement

is added to the vaults for seismic protection in order to deal with Kigali's moderate-risk earthquake zone. The vaults work in compression, allowing the structure to be extremely thin, with the largest vault spanning over fifty-two feet (sixteen meters).

Simple, efficient concrete tables are added to more enclosed spaces—the service areas, changing rooms, offices, and a restaurant. Low-carbon, agro-waste fired, locally made bricks are used to define edges and spaces. Local broken granite and slate, as well as clay tiles, are used for flooring.

TYPE
SPORT & RECREATION:
STADIUM / ARENA

WINNER
POPULAR CHOICE

PROJECT STATUS
CONCEPT

YEAR
2017

FIRM LOCATION
MADRID
SPAIN

Tropicalia
Côte d'Opale, France

Coldefy & Associés
Architectes Urbanistes

TYPE
SPORT & RECREATION:
UNBUILT SPORT
& RECREATION

WINNER
JURY
POPULAR CHOICE

PROJECT STATUS
CONCEPT

YEAR
2018

FIRM LOCATION
LILLE
FRANCE

French architecture firm Coldefy & Associés Architectes Urbanistes—in collaboration with energy company Dalkia—unveiled plans for a huge tropical greenhouse to be built in the north of France.

Named Tropicalia, the 215,280-square-foot (twenty thousand square meters) structure will be the largest of its kind, featuring a tropical forest, a turtle beach, a waterfall, an Olympic-sized pool for Amazonian fish, and a long walking trail, all designed to make it a harmonious haven. There will also be an auditorium, a restaurant, a bed and breakfast, and a scientific area complete with a conference room, laboratory, and clinic.

To make sure the project is as environmentally friendly as possible,

ETFE plastic technology is being utilized in a "double-dome" structure, allowing UV light to pass through while controlling thermal conditions inside. A third layer of ETFE will be placed underneath the structure, which will itself be partially embedded into the landscape, allowing natural thermal heat to be captured. It is to be assumed that the project will be energy self-sufficient.

The scope of the project requires a location around the city that allows a generous deployment and the capacity to accommodate large groups of visitors. In contrast to a megastructure, the building does not create a break with its environment but rises to welcome the surrounding fauna and flora.

The World's Biggest Bicycle Parking
Utrecht, The Netherlands
Ector Hoogstad Architecten

Historically, the Dutch have always been fervent cyclists. More and more public transport hubs will have amenities for cyclists, as increasing numbers of people favor the combination of cycling and public transport over cars.

As the Utrecht Central station area is undergoing a major makeover, a new public street aimed mainly at pedestrians is being inserted. It rises by means of ninety-eight-foot-wide (thirty meters) stairs to a level of twenty feet (six meters) to widen into a square, marked by an enormous iconic canopy, where the entrance of the station is situated.

A three-story bicycle parking area is situated underneath the square. It has been designed with three aims in mind: convenience, speed, and safety. In order to achieve this, cyclists are able to pedal all the way up to their parking slot. The parking lanes branch off the cycle paths, to ensure pedestrians never cross with cyclists. Modestly sloping ramps connect the parking areas on different levels, and electronic signals indicate the position of free parking slots.

TYPE
TRANSPORTATION:
TRANSPORTATION
INFRASTRUCTURE

WINNER
JURY

PROJECT STATUS
BUILT

YEAR
2018

FIRM LOCATION
ROTTERDAM
THE NETHERLANDS

Rainbow Bridge
Long Beach, CA, USA
SPF:architects

Located in Long Beach, California, the Rainbow Bridge was opened to the public in December 2017. Over a four-year period, from RFP (request for proposal) to the end of construction, the project underwent dramatic changes in both purpose and design. Two major venues in Long Beach, the Convention Center and Performing Arts Center, required a connection that would allow visitors to circulate freely between the two locations.

The finished project is a spectacular six-hundred-foot (180 meters) pedestrian bridge consisting of seventy-six custom-welded bent-steel ribs framing the top, and approximately 1,200 cubic yards of poured-in-place concrete shaping the base. The bridge canopy features 3,500 color-changing LED node lights, one hundred downlights, and seventy floodlights, all of which can be programmed to music to create different effects.

SPF:architects worked closely with Carl Stahl Architektur to create the custom, three-piece, stainless-steel node clip that allows for the bridge's LED wiring to attach to the canopy.

The Rainbow Bridge draws from Long Beach's history as a dynamic seaside town with its active port and local attractions. The bridge is formally conceived as an abstraction of a breaking wave with a deck that is composed of multifarious strands or eddies of elements that typify a boardwalk environment.

TYPE
TRANSPORTATION:
TRANSPORTATION
INFRASTRUCTURE

WINNER
POPULAR CHOICE

PROJECT STATUS
BUILT

YEAR
2017

FIRM LOCATION
CULVER CITY, CA
USA

Turanganui Bridge
Gisborne, New Zealand

Monk Mackenzie

TYPE
TRANSPORTATION:
UNBUILT TRANSPORTATION

WINNER
JURY

PROJECT STATUS
CONCEPT

YEAR
2018

FIRM LOCATION
AUCKLAND
NEW ZEALAND

This project celebrates the exact point of the first contact between British explorer Captain James Cook and New Zealand Māori in 1769. The project is situated in Gisborne, New Zealand, and is located in the Turanganui River on a rock known as Te Toka a Taiau/Taiao.

It is embodied in the form through two entities that emerge from the landscape, meeting at a delicate apex above the river. The form is muscular at the base, tapering to a thin section at the moment of connection. The bridge deck widens in the plan at the apex above the river to act as a meeting place and dramatic viewing deck out to sea.

The form of the bridge uses a sweeping elliptical line—creating a trajectory for the eye to follow—resulting in a dynamic and highly expressive silhouette.

The geometry of the bridge was designed to rise naturally and effortlessly from the landscape. This was designed by creating a bridge alignment and elevation that emerges tangentially from the slipway and ground. The steps and seating areas at the base of the bridge emerge from the ground and slipway as if carved from the landscape and are shaped to naturally anchor the bridge.

Beibu Gulf International Oceanic Transit Center
Beihai, China

GOA

TYPE
TRANSPORTATION:
UNBUILT TRANSPORTATION

WINNER
POPULAR CHOICE

PROJECT STATUS
CONCEPT

YEAR
2018

FIRM LOCATION
HANGZHOU
CHINA

Beibu Gulf International Oceanic Transit Center is located at the south end of downtown Beihai, Guangxi Zhuang Autonomous Region, and closely adjoins the Xunliao Bay at the portal of the Beibu Gulf. It is an important offshore civil shipping hub for traveling from Beihai to the Weizhou Island and Haikou.

The project consists of a shipping terminal, marine hotel, marine culture-themed commercial street, health and fitness center, and several other functional sectors. The shipping terminal is located in the southernmost area of the site, adjacent to the harbor basin and directly facing the seaward channel.

The building employs a planar layout of independently arranged waiting halls in pairs, which can be separated and combined as needed to effectively respond to the service demands of shipping lines in low and high seasons. The design technique can control building scale and was combined with local vegetation characteristics to create a new-generation transportation building with a tropical flavor.

Swisshouse XXXII
Rossa, Switzerland

Davide Macullo Architects

The Swisshouse XXXII in Rossa represents a constant commitment to build with respect for the places we inhabit and to make every effort to help advance our understanding of modern civilization. Rossa is a place of memory where civilization is based on simplicity. The task is to continue the love for this land through humble but enduring gestures. Building in this context requires taking cues from the past and following the pace of a place that catalyzes complex energies.

The cross in vertical projection, the rounding of the edges, and the simple torsion of the roof allow for a dynamic that reinterprets the archetype of the house. Each aperture is calibrated and oriented toward selected views of the surrounding landscape. The basement features reinforced concrete, while the upper volume is made entirely of wood, reinterpreting the traditional construction type of the Alps.

TYPE
CONCEPTS — PLUS:
ARCHITECTURE + ART

WINNER
JURY

PROJECT STATUS
BUILT

YEAR
2017

FIRM LOCATION
LUGANO
SWITZERLAND

MIST Hot Spring Resort
Henan, China

Department of ARCHITECTURE Co.

Designers always want to enhance a site's uniqueness. However, at MIST, the best attribute is hidden down below. The design challenge was how to capture the beauty of the invisible water found underground. The final inspiration came from the beauty of the hot spring steam itself—the project attempts to heighten its surreal and mystic beauty, in all design aspects, from master layout to architecture and its interior space.

Large site-specific installations exploring natural phenomena relating to mist and water were especially designed and installed throughout the resort as the main elements that tie the entire experience together.

In the lobby and bar, an installation made of hundreds of layers of clear and colored crystals is inspired by a spectrum of light passing through hot steam, which can be viewed differently depending on position of the viewers. The interior space is kept monochrome with color accents in crystals in the installation and in floor lighting sculptures. Color-changing light at the edge of the acrylic planes gives different moods to different time of the day. In the ballroom, a matrix of forty-five thousand plus acrylic rings forms a semitransparent, irregular cloudlike shape.

TYPE
CONCEPTS — PLUS:
ARCHITECTURE + ART

WINNER
JURY

PROJECT STATUS
BUILT

YEAR
2018

FIRM LOCATION
BANGKOK
THAILAND

LEGO House
Billund, Denmark

BIG – Bjarke Ingels Group

TYPE
CONCEPTS — PLUS:
ARCHITECTURE + BRANDING

WINNER
JURY
POPULAR CHOICE

PROJECT STATUS
BUILT

YEAR
2017

FIRM LOCATION
BROOKLYN, NY
USA

LEGO House is a literal manifestation of the infinite possibilities of the LEGO brick. Aligned to the LEGO Group's philosophy, LEGO House is conceived as a three-dimensional village of interlocking and overlapping buildings and spaces. Each space can be designed and used independently.

At the ground level, the LEGO square is energized by an urban character, welcoming locals and visitors to the café, restaurant, LEGO store, and conference facilities. Above the square, the first and second floors include four play zones arranged by color and programmed with activities that represent a certain aspect of a child's learning: red is creative, blue is cognitive, green is social, and yellow is emotional. Guests of all ages can have an immersive and interactive experience and express their imagination. The top of the building is crowned by the Masterpiece Gallery made of the iconic LEGO bricks that showcase art beneath eight circular skylights that resemble the studs of the brick.

Like the golden ratio, the proportions of the brick are nested in the geometries of everything man-made in the building, from the glazed ceramic tiles in the steps and walls to the overall twenty-one-block scheme.

Intuit Marine Way Building
Mountain View, CA, USA

WRNS Studio and Clive Wilkinson Architects

TYPE
CONCEPTS — PLUS:
ARCHITECTURE +
COLLABORATION

WINNER
JURY

PROJECT STATUS
BUILT

YEAR
2017

FIRM LOCATIONS
SAN FRANCISCO, CA
USA

LOS ANGELES, CA
USA

The planning and geometry of the Marine Way Building (MWB), featuring 185,400 square feet (17,200 square meters) over four floors, can be understood as low, wide, connected, and flexible—a strategy that addresses the specific programmatic and collaborative needs of Intuit's employees. The large floor plates, which accommodate a variety of places for people to collaborate, concentrate, socialize, and reflect, are organized into human-scaled neighborhoods and connected by clear circulation. A café, living rooms, bike facilities, showers, and terraces spin off of a highly visible atrium that welcomes up to five hundred people at a time and opens out onto the campus's main internal street. The four-story main atrium space draws activity from the east and west sides of the campus and serves as the center of the MWB and the greater Intuit community.

Each landing and bleacher stair along the atrium connects directly to a large "living room" with pantry functions and generous interteam collaborative work space. This variety of programmatic functions along the perimeter of the atrium helps generate a consistent buzz of activity throughout the workday.

SINBIN
Portland, OR, USA

Skylab

TYPE
CONCEPTS – PLUS:
ARCHITECTURE +
COLLABORATION

WINNER
POPULAR CHOICE

PROJECT STATUS
BUILT

YEAR
2017

FIRM LOCATION
PORTLAND, OR
USA

SINBIN is a creative house balancing both natural and built environments. At its core, the space inspires action and activity. It is purpose-built for playing, making, and collaboration of all types. Inspired by Gordon Matta-Clark's iconic *Building Cuts*, two existing warehouses, totaling 9,500 square feet (880 square meters), were cut into and modified. Peeling back the roof of one and slicing into the other, the warehouses are remixed, repurposed, and fused with the new building's geometric pinwheel framework, creating a space that seamlessly blends the old and new.

The studio environments on the ground floor are places to make art, record music, perform, and skate. The private owner and artist-in-residence units occupy the second and third floors, with green roofs and outdoor yards reintroducing one-third of the site back to green space to manage stormwater. Circulation and flow throughout removes traditional barriers between activities to experience the influence of other spaces, actions, and making. A geometric interplay of space plays out through editing the existing buildings while creating new forms that emerge out of the existing framework.

Chaoyang Future School
Beijing, China
Crossboundaries

Chaoyang Future School seeks to integrate architectural reuse with pedagogical innovation, thereby adding to the ongoing life span of an existing campus and the restoration of its educational relevance and purpose. The project strongly incorporates the use of color throughout the facade, landscape, and interior to provide identity and intuitive orientation.

The renovated facades replace deteriorating, rust-colored stucco with clean white surfaces. Preserving the rhythm of the original fenestrations, square frames project out at varying lengths, undulating in response to the corresponding spatial activities within. Washed in colors inspired by the rich deciduous and evergreen flora of the the site, the frames sustain the liveliness of the outdoor spaces and bring them deep into the buildings. Green hues outline the public face of the campus, subtly fading to yellow before warming to a deep red as they reach the campus center.

Behind each facade, interior spaces use corresponding colors to relay their programmatic identity. The vibrant, scarlet red Art Center becomes the gravitational heart of campus; warm, rich oranges mark the canteen and café; lively yellows gild faculty spaces, and bright greens invigorate the classrooms.

In the Learning Center, small-scale interventions dissolve the spatial boundaries of the buildings' rigid structure and uniformity, producing collaborative learning spaces bolstered by user-defined furniture.

TYPE
CONCEPTS — PLUS:
ARCHITECTURE + COLOR

WINNER
JURY

PROJECT STATUS
BUILT

YEAR
2017

FIRM LOCATION
BEIJING
CHINA

The Street
Mathura, India

Sanjay Puri Architects

Taking a cue from the old city streets of Mathura, India, where this project is located, this eight-hundred-room student hostel offers organically expanding spaces. Designed in five linear blocks, the built volumes twist and turn along their length on a wedge-shaped site.

The orientation of the buildings is complete with a view of large north-facing gardens overlooking a vast playground toward the north. Each room in the hostel is equipped with a wedge-shaped, north-facing bay window on the outside and ventilators toward the internal corridor, facilitating both cross ventilation and light

throughout the year. Two focal areas created at the end of the building house cafeterias, games rooms, and gyms opening into north-facing gardens and terraces. All the public spaces are large volumes with twenty-foot-high (six meters) ceilings.

These factors result in an energy-efficient building that minimizes heat gain in response to the hot climate. Rainwater harvesting, water recycling, and usage of solar panels make it more energy-efficient, along with the orientation and facilitation of natural ventilation.

TYPE
CONCEPTS — PLUS:
ARCHITECTURE + COLOR

WINNER
POPULAR CHOICE

PROJECT STATUS
BUILT

YEAR
2017

FIRM LOCATION
MUMBAI
INDIA

The Storefront Theater
Lyons, NE, USA

Matthew Mazzotta

The Storefront Theater is a unique event space that transforms Main Street into an outdoor theater by using an abandoned freestanding storefront wall in downtown Lyons, Nebraska, as its site. The wall is modified with two hydraulic pump arms so that the awning and false front fold down over the sidewalk with the push of a button, providing seating for one hundred guests. Both the seats and the screen retract and disappear when not in use, giving the impression that there is nothing unusual in this town, leaving only word-of-mouth accounts for inquiring visitors.

The project began when artist Matthew Mazzotta, who was invited to organize a project in Lyons, asked people from the community to join him in an outdoor living room placed on Main Street as a way to provoke discussion and capture stories and ideas. As the community pulled together to build the retractable theater, a local retired postman who dabbles in moviemaking asked to be part of the project. To help the amateur filmmaker realize his dream of creating a feature film, over one hundred people in this 850-person town volunteered by following his shooting schedule and showing up in period costumes and their vintage cars.

TYPE
CONCEPTS — PLUS:
ARCHITECTURE + COMMUNITY

WINNER
JURY

PROJECT STATUS
BUILT

YEAR
2016

FIRM LOCATION
CANTON, OH
USA

Habitat for Orphan Girls
Khansar, Iran

ZAV Architects

Strategic decisions drove the architecture of a shelter in the city of Khansar for orphaned girls. In response to the financial limitations of the project, an austere and honest approach had to be adopted. All superfluous layers of finishing and ornamentation were eliminated as a result.

It is hard to exercise one's rights in choosing one's lifestyle as an orphaned girl in a male-dominated religious city such as Khansar. In an attempt to critique the status quo—even though the architecture of the shelter adopts an introverted typology in response to concerns about security—the facade of the project transforms into a medium that allows the building to close down or open up to the city as the girls require or desire, capitalizing on the hand-operated exterior curtains of the balconies.

The site of the project is located within the historic fabric of the city. The project was proposed to the owner of the site by the design team. Every urban heritage has the potential to initiate financial prosperity for the city and its inhabitants. As such, the past of the city becomes the future of its orphaned inhabitants.

TYPE
CONCEPTS — PLUS:
ARCHITECTURE + COMMUNITY

WINNER
POPULAR CHOICE

PROJECT STATUS
CONCEPT

YEAR
2016

FIRM LOCATION
TORONTO, ON
CAN

Rong Cultural Center
Hormoz Island, Iran

ZAV Architects

TYPE
CONCEPTS – PLUS:
ARCHITECTURE +
HUMANITARIANISM

WINNER
JURY

PROJECT STATUS
BUILT

YEAR
2017

FIRM LOCATION
TORONTO, ON
CAN

Hormoz Island in the Persian Gulf is economically stressed and has a history of consecutive failures when it comes to environmental issues. Hormoz red soil has long been a matter of tension, and it still is perceived as the plundering of the island's natural resources by many locals.

To tackle this problem, multidisciplinary brainstorming workshops were held in a community center, which was set up temporarily to gain the participation of Hormozians. In conclusion, a cultural center containing tourist information, a café, and an event management center was decided upon. Rong is the name chosen for this complex.

After consideration of local and international case studies, the design team came to the conclusion that the rammed-earth system could be appropriated and retrofitted with more contemporary solutions to be used for Rong. The adopted sandbag technology was combined with a steel structure covered with cement. Rong is a permanent urban space, which exists in harmony with the island's geomorphology and appears as an icon at the entry port of the island, bringing pride to Hormoz.

Dabao Primary School and Community Cultural Centre
Dabao, China

Project Mingde (the University of Hong Kong) and Elisabeth Lee

Dabao village is remotely situated within the scenic mountain range of Guangxi province in China. This isolated settlement provides home to around 110 families of an ethnic minority group called the Yaos, who have their own distinct dialect and culture.

Due to their seclusion and poverty, the village lacked a safe environment for its children to learn. Thus, the Dabao project aimed at providing the Yaos with a primary school, which at the same time could serve as a community center. The design and construction processes involved an active dialogue between Dabao villagers and the team—a reciprocal exchange in culture, knowledge, and skills.

The building is situated within the paddy fields on the mountains of Dabao. The design concept is structured around the use of layers of walls, addressing the challenges originated from the steep topography of the site. The use of different diameters and lengths of bamboo tubes responds adequately to the different light requirements of the rooms for their respective functions.

The main level of the building houses two classrooms and a community library. An outdoor playground and gathering area is located on the second level with access to the roof, accessible for the children to play and other villagers to rest.

TYPE
CONCEPTS — PLUS:
ARCHITECTURE +
HUMANITARIANISM

WINNER
POPULAR CHOICE

PROJECT STATUS
BUILT

YEAR
2015

FIRM LOCATION
HONG KONG

Issa Megaron
Vis, Croatia
Proarh

TYPE
CONCEPTS – PLUS:
ARCHITECTURE + LANDSCAPE

WINNER
JURY

PROJECT STATUS
BUILT

YEAR
2016

FIRM LOCATION
ZAGREB
CROATIA

The Issa Megaron project deals with questions regarding the context of the site. Given the Mediterranean location, the architects conceived the design of the house by the system of the Socrates Megaron (as the first passive house), reinterpreting the ancient traditional stone drywalls and creating a new rural man-made topography.

The assignment was to design a house for a temporary family retreat on a site without infrastructure, and at the same time completely satisfy the needs of the users. The complete lack of infrastructure and general inaccessibility meant that self-sustainability was a priority and the only solution for the completion of the project. The house is designed with natural cooling and ventilation systems, rainwater exploitation, solar panels,

and other elaborate ways of harnessing natural resources, enabling the facility to function as a place to live.

The house is envisioned as a dug-in volume, a residential pocket between the stretches of space-forming walls and an artificial grotto. It consists of two levels: sleeping quarters/lounge on the first floor, and a downstairs dining/kitchen/lounge area, which open to both covered and uncovered terraces and a pool deck. All the bearing elements are made of reinforced concrete. Stone from the site was used for the cladding of the facade.

Fleinvær Refugium
Fleinvær, Norway

TYIN tegnestue
Architects and
Rintala Eggertsson
Architects

TYPE
CONCEPTS — PLUS:
ARCHITECTURE + LANDSCAPE

WINNER
POPULAR CHOICE

PROJECT STATUS
BUILT

YEAR
2017

FIRM LOCATIONS
TRONDHEIM
NORWAY

OSLO
NORWAY

Fleinvær Refugium is an artist residency located in the remote archipelago of Fleinvær in northern Norway. The project came about after composer/musician Håvard Lund contacted TYIN tegnestue Architects, which in turn contacted Rintala Eggertsson Architects to do a collaborative effort to design and build the project. During the first phase of the design, it became evident to everyone involved that a piece of nature so vulnerable, delicate, and architectonic had to be saved from excavators and demolition machines.

As a consequence, each of the functions was given buildings of its own: the sauna on a pier by the waterfront, the main cabins at the bottom of the hill, and the work space at a recess in the hillside. To complete the composition with a reference to the vernacular of the Sami indigenous people in the area, a small cabin on the top of a column was designed.

From the fairly pragmatic approach to the organization of the cluster of buildings, the team moved forward in four separate design/build workshops to manufacture the structures. A natural consequence of the design concerns was the choice of wood as a main building material: it is sustainable and carbon binding, and can be crafted directly on-site.

Adventurous Global School
Battambang, Cambodia

OOA – Occident Orient Atelier

There are many meaningful village school projects in the world. To go further, OOA's charity school project transforms the construction site itself into a learning kit. As such, the school building not only provides a traditional lecture space, but also functions as a proactive space for learning design, construction, and spatial creativity. During construction, students took part in some of the manageable design processes.

The building envelope incorporates spatial flexibilities for its end users, allowing for the reconfiguration of openings, shelves, and lockers. The wall is a double-layer steel frame with local wood plates allowing for storage and vertical circulation. The doors can slide to either connect or disconnect spaces. On the ground floor, classrooms are seamlessly connected with adjacent houses and fields, thereby catering to different events, learning activities, and class sizes. The relation between interior and exterior can thus be customized by different users in the future. It is a welcoming space in which other villagers and students can easily see what is going on and join the classes if desired.

Answering to the local topology, the levitated concrete structure mitigates flooding problems while also providing a traditional Cambodian ground-floor open space. Consciously, the architects made use of the local construction methodology, thereby empowering people with local skills.

TYPE
CONCEPTS – PLUS:
ARCHITECTURE + LEARNING

WINNER
JURY
POPULAR CHOICE

PROJECT STATUS
BUILT

YEAR
2017

FIRM LOCATION
HONG KONG

At the Table with Rapitea
Mexico City, Mexico

EDAA and Yupica

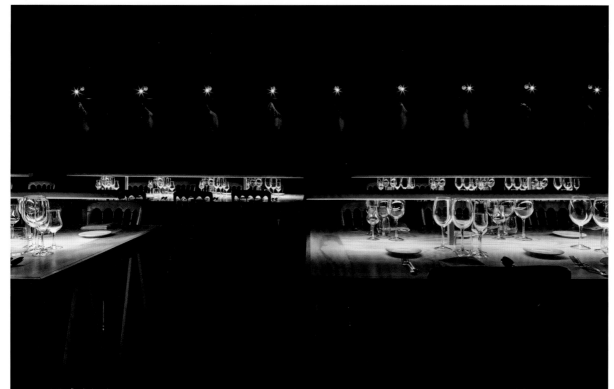

At the Table with Rapitea is a three-day ephemeral restaurant hosting 120 people during Mexico City's most prestigious culinary pop-up event, Millesime Mexico by Millesime World. This is a collaborative work by Mexico City-based architecture practice EDAA and Japanese multimedia artist Yupica, in which visual and culinary art, as well as sound pieces by Chimi Jo, are blended into a unique experience of sober but complex quality.

Just as Yupica extrapolates food to the art field, the chef transforms the most basic food into a culinary event dealing with symbolic references. EDAA did not simply design a restaurant but a common space for delight.

Millesime Mexico's 2017 slogan was "Earth: Sustainable Culinary." The architects' proposal was based on the premise of sustainability, meaning that all materials should be easily reusable without major industrial processing being necessary. The design and construction elements included tables built from plywood for a concrete formwork, table lighting from commercial steel sections, a black carpet for flooring and black paint on the walls, a plafond from construction shade cloth, and art by Yupica.

TYPE
CONCEPTS — PLUS:
ARCHITECTURE + LIGHT

WINNER
JURY

PROJECT STATUS
BUILT

YEAR
2017

FIRM LOCATION
MEXICO CITY
MEXICO

King Abdullah Petroleum Studies and Research Center
Riyadh, Saudi Arabia
Office for Visual Interaction

TYPE
CONCEPTS — PLUS:
ARCHITECTURE + LIGHT

WINNER
POPULAR CHOICE

PROJECT STATUS
BUILT

YEAR
2017

FIRM LOCATION
NEW YORK, NY
USA

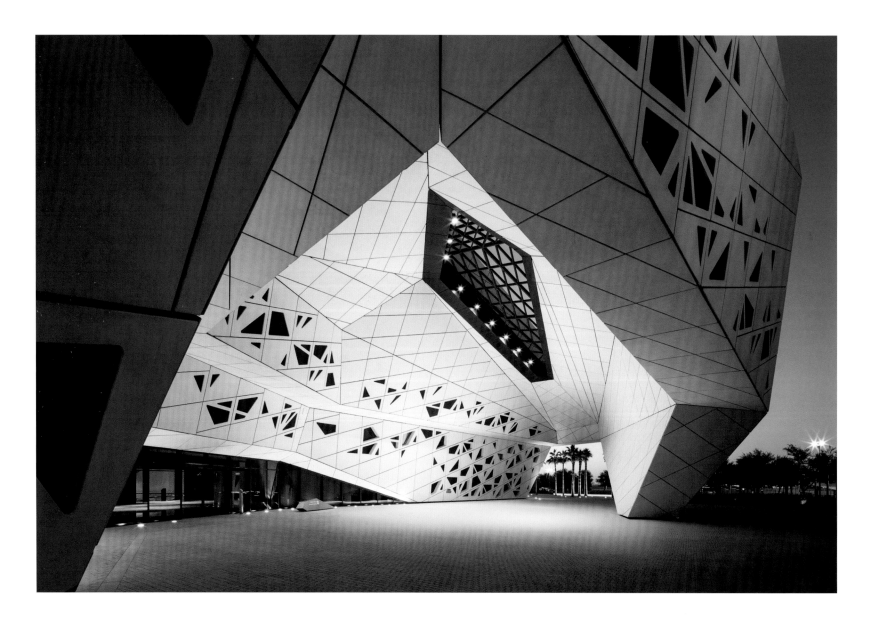

From competition entry to reality, this multibuilding campus is a three-dimensional, parametric sculpture located in Riyadh, Saudi Arabia. Lighting creates the central focal point of the project's nighttime identity, glowing and softly radiating throughout the site.

The site is a virtual microcity, exceeding 5,382,000 square feet (500,000 square meters) characterized by innovative design, featuring a series of interlocking, cellular structures woven together by an open-air central plaza.

Each building profile of the architectural dunelike forms has a different height and contour. There are no right angles or identical sections, resulting in highly atypical facades.

A strategic lighting vocabulary was developed utilizing internal glow, vertical illumination, contrast, and silhouettes to articulate the dynamic forms. In-grade linear luminaires are positioned strategically to anchor specific facades while keeping in mind distant viewing angles and the cohesiveness of the overall design of the complex. At night, interior volumes appear chiseled with light to enhance the sharp, angular design. As a spiritual center, the Musalla—used for outdoor prayer—is a symbolic embodiment of light, with illumination as a transformative element in the emotional and experiential journey for worshippers.

Tiny Pavilion Vught
Vught, The Netherlands
studio PROTOTYPE

Studio PROTOTYPE completed a tiny pavilion located in the garden of a villa. The villa was built in a parklike environment at the Rondeweg in Vught in the 1930s.

Conceptually, the contextual character of the park has been continued within the site of the villa. The two pavilions added as part of the interior park elegantly communicate with the existing house. Although they have their own identity and materiality, the pavilions form a unity with the overall concept. It is the first of the two pavilions that has been completed.

The main structure of the tiny pavilion consists of a facility block, which is strategically positioned within a free space. The block functions as a servant's space and contains a cupboard bed, pantry, bathroom, and fireplace. The hipped roof, clad with copper sheets, has been hollowed on the inside in several places. As a result, an interior roofscape is created that enhances the specific spatial qualities of every space. Iroko wood window frames were used for the all-glass facade, which results in a strong relation between the interior and the surrounding garden.

TYPE
CONCEPTS — PLUS:
ARCHITECTURE +
LIVING SMALL

WINNER
JURY

PROJECT STATUS
BUILT

YEAR
2017

FIRM LOCATION
AMSTERDAM
THE NETHERLANDS

Kasita
Austin, TX, USA

Kasita

At Kasita, it is believed that every aspect of one's living space should make life simpler and fuller. That is why the home has been reinvented here to support the way life is actually lived. Created in over one thousand design hours, Kasita is an award-winning microhome that is perfect for those who want to live simply, or for a homeowner who desires some extra space. Whether for a guest house, an elderly person, or an additional rental, this home offers enough space for everything that is needed and for nothing that is not.

TYPE
CONCEPTS — PLUS:
ARCHITECTURE +
LIVING SMALL

WINNER
POPULAR CHOICE

PROJECT STATUS
BUILT

YEAR
2017

FIRM LOCATION
AUSTIN, TX
USA

Champ-du-Château, Architectural Visualization
Geneva, Switzerland

Brick Visual

The architects created a movie as well as still images for the Champ-du-Château project, which was a competition proposal designed by Favre & Guth. Parametric architecture truly inspired the architects in the creative process, finally leading them to show compositions that are unique and display the building in an unconventional yet highly engaging way—both in motion picture format and still images.

TYPE
CONCEPTS — PLUS:
ARCHITECTURE +
MODELS & RENDERING

WINNER
JURY
POPULAR CHOICE

PROJECT STATUS
CONCEPT

YEAR
2016

FIRM LOCATION
BUDAPEST
HUNGARY

Kengo Kuma Teahouse
Vancouver, BC, Canada

Ema Peter Photography

Nestled in a delicate moss and pebble landscape, the Teahouse is a space for stillness and quiet amid Vancouver's busy downtown core. The Teahouse embodies the Japanese philosophy of *chado*, which implies an essential way of life, one that is closely aligned to the metaphysical notion of *being*. At the most refined level, the ceremony takes place in the tea house. The solitude of the tea ceremony evokes a deep meditative stillness, bringing the beholder's awareness back to the most basic level of consciousness.

Usually, tea houses are small, simple wooden buildings, located in the gardens or grounds of private homes or on grounds of temples, museums, and parks. Instead of designing a closed wooden structure, Kengo Kuma, the renowned Japanese architect also designing a residential tower in Vancouver, used steel and glass to frame expansive views over Coal Harbour. Local Douglas fir wood was used in place of traditional Japanese cedar. The shoji screens were covered in Japanese washi paper, and the tatami mats were handmade in Japan. Carefully detailed and thoughtfully crafted, the Teahouse is a modern interpretation of a traditional Japanese structure.

TYPE
CONCEPTS — PLUS:
ARCHITECTURE +
PHOTOGRAPHY & VIDEO

WINNER
JURY
POPULAR CHOICE

PROJECT STATUS
CONCEPT

YEAR
2017

FIRM LOCATION
VANCOUVER, BC
CANADA

Cherokee Residence
Los Angeles, CA, USA

Reddymade Architecture
& Design and LivingHomes

TYPE
CONCEPTS — PLUS:
ARCHITECTURE + PREFAB

WINNER
JURY
POPULAR CHOICE

PROJECT STATUS
CONCEPT

YEAR
2017

FIRM LOCATIONS
NEW YORK, NY
USA

SANTA MONICA, CA
USA

The house is composed of six modules on two levels that create the primary living spaces, with a custom-built stair volume, garage, and guest annex. Based on a design that Ray Kappe had created for LivingHomes, the midcentury Modern–inspired design blurs the boundary between exterior and interior spaces while maintaining a strong sense of privacy. The design is customized to fit into a steeply sloping site with an infinity pool that drops off at the rear.

An exterior garden divides the home into distinct zones, private for bedrooms and baths, and public for kitchen, living, and dining spaces. The master suite and private deck is oriented toward the pool and the spectacular sunsets.

Utilizing prefabricated construction methods for the majority of the home minimizes neighborhood disruption and reduces overall site construction time and cost. Modular and site construction of the home occur simultaneously, allowing the home to be delivered and assembled on-site in a single day, leaving landscaping, pool, and remaining finish work to be completed postinstallation.

The use of overhangs emphasizes the horizontality of the plan while doubling as passive cooling for interior comfort. Exposed steel frames, cedar, and glass keep the exterior palette simple, durable, and timeless.

The Dovecote-Granary
Ponte de Lima, Portugal

Tiago do Vale Architects

TYPE
CONCEPTS — PLUS:
ARCHITECTURE +
PRESERVATION

WINNER
JURY
POPULAR CHOICE

PROJECT STATUS
CONCEPT

YEAR
2017

FIRM LOCATION
BRAGA
PORTUGAL

The starting point for this project was two traditional northern Portugal maize granaries standing over granite bases originally built in the late-nineteenth century. A common roof—under which there was a dovecote—united them. The space between the two granaries was used to dry cereals, with two huge basculating panels controlling the ventilation.

The granary's rotten wood pieces allowed for a full documentation of the design and constructive techniques of the building from when it was last used, opening the doors for a piece-by-piece reconstruction. These circumstances implied not only reconstruction but also transformation, giving form to the theme of the project. The result is an elementary rebuild of the Dovecote-Granary, including an intricate redesign of carpentry details and a limited set of surgical interventions that will allow for its safe and renewed use.

The Dovecote-Granary is now a sanctuary among the tree canopies, an iconic vernacular shape in the rural landscape of the Minho region—and the experience of dancing leaf shadows, the gentle crossing breeze, and chirping birds in a late summer afternoon defines its new purpose, function, and use.

Alila Yangshuo
Guangxi, China

Horizontal Space Design
and Vector Architects

The Alila Yangshuo hotel is situated between two mountains that make the area around China's Guangxi region a popular destination for tourists looking to take in the picturesque scenery. The designers were tasked with the creation of a hotel on the site of a disused sugar mill, constructed in the 1960s and comprising a cluster of buildings alongside a truss used for loading sugar cane onto boats.

The project involved retaining and repurposing the existing structures, as well as introducing new accommodation buildings that complement the existing industrial aesthetic. The structure designed by Dong Gong of Vector Architects and the interior design by Ju Bin of Horizontal Space Design aim to emphasize the connection between old and new. The original buildings now contain amenities including the hotel's reception, a café, a bar, a multipurpose hall, a gallery, and a library, all arranged around a reflecting pond and with a sunken plaza at the very center of the complex.

TYPE
CONCEPTS — PLUS:
ARCHITECTURE + RENOVATION

WINNER
JURY

PROJECT STATUS
BUILT

YEAR
2017

FIRM LOCATIONS
SHENZHEN
CHINA

BEIJING
CHINA

Villa F / The Off-the-Grid House in the Central Highlands of Germany
Titmaringhausen, Germany
Christoph Hesse Architects

Villa F is an off-the-grid house in the central highlands of Germany. Energy-efficiency and protection of the environment have formed the main concerns of the design. Furthermore, the client stipulated a round house as an additional requirement. The main reason for this was that from an energy-efficient point of view, the surface and volume proportion would have been ideal. However, since it is rather hard to live in a sphere, the client ultimately decided on a cylindrical shape.

The building comprises two floors. There are bedrooms on the first floor, while the loftlike second floor features living rooms and a whirlpool with a view to the landscape. The client-farmer's close relation to nature also shows in the design of the facade, which was built with stones from a nearby creek and leads to a continuity in the development of the entire building.

TYPE
CONCEPTS — PLUS:
ARCHITECTURE +
SUSTAINABILITY

WINNER
JURY

PROJECT STATUS
BUILT

YEAR
2016

FIRM LOCATION
KORBACH
GERMANY

Somjai House
Surat Thani, Thailand
NPDAstudio

The architectural design of Somjai House aims to explore new taste and creativity within traditional Thai architecture, based on specific local conditions. Somjai House is located in the middle of a tropical coconut plantation on Phangan Island. The front of the building was conceived with open angles to allow a full view of the sea. To protect the building from south-facing sunlight, a cantilever concept was used. On the top, a tilted roof lets the rain flow through the bathroom before ending in a fish pond.

The building consists of bedrooms, bathrooms, and a pantry. The main hall of the building serves as a flexible, multi-purpose space. It can be used as a living space or transformed into a yoga area. The upper deck was designed to provide panoramic views of the surrounding coconut plantation, the sea, Samui Island, and the hills.

In order to make the building stand out from the green of the coconut plantation and the blue of the sea, red has been used as the main color. Due to their cooling properties, brick and polished concrete were used to protect the house from heat gain. The project implemented local construction expertise, with a thin iron staircase showing off the craftsmanship of local workmen.

TYPE
CONCEPTS — PLUS:
ARCHITECTURE +
SUSTAINABILITY

WINNER
POPULAR CHOICE

PROJECT STATUS
BUILT

YEAR
2015

FIRM LOCATION
BANGKOK
THAILAND

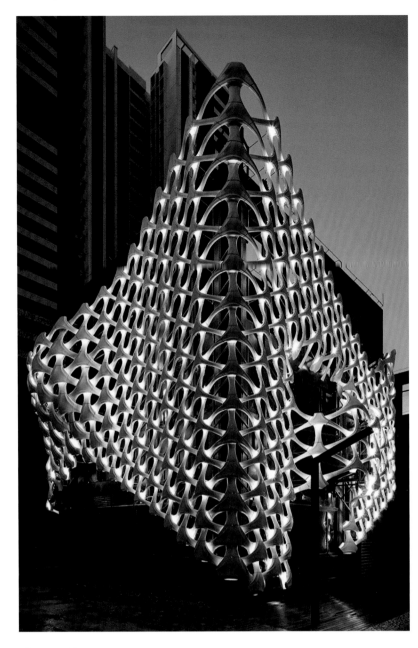

Arachne is a digital architectural endeavor that redefines an ordinary building with 3-D printed components. To reflect its literal title, Arachne was designed and installed as spatially intertwined lattices that cling onto the building and form a curtain wall mechanism.

The initial volume gift wrapped by Arachne is a three-floor building. The brief was to cover the main facades, which face an important public square. An advanced 3-D printing technology was selected to meet this requirement.

Geometrically, the hexagon was chosen as a starting point to develop the form. Three groups of threads are braided to create an interwoven network. This network is eloquently forced to deform in locations where it intersects with the

building masses, such as the balcony and the rain roof.

There are over two thousand components, which can be categorized into two types: the hexagon joints and the connecting struts, which took fifty large FDM printers and more than four months to fabricate. There are particle lights located on the second layer, which subdue the structure with a backlit appearance. The installation was such a unique design that every single piece has a designated location.

Arachne
Foshan, China

Archit-Solution Workshop

TYPE
CONCEPTS — PLUS:
ARCHITECTURE +
TECHNOLOGY

WINNER
JURY

PROJECT STATUS
BUILT

YEAR
2017

FIRM LOCATION
BEIJING
CHINA

Shirley Ryan AbilityLab
Chicago, IL, USA

HDR, Gensler, and Clive Wilkinson Architects

TYPE
CONCEPTS — PLUS:
ARCHITECTURE +
TECHNOLOGY

WINNER
POPULAR CHOICE

PROJECT STATUS
BUILT

YEAR
2016

FIRM LOCATION
LOS ANGELES, CA
USA

The Shirley Ryan AbilityLab, formerly the Rehabilitation Institute of Chicago, is the number one destination for adults and children with the most complex conditions—from brain and spinal cord injuries to stroke, cancer, and amputation. The client's vision was to reshape the future of rehabilitation and transform how discoveries are applied to advance human ability.

Concepts integral to translational health drove planning and design: research does not simply coexist with care but is integrated into the clinical environment, engaging patients in the process. Each of five ability labs—Think + Speak, Legs + Walking, Arms + Hands, Strength + Endurance, and Pediatrics—act as the "front stage" for patients to work with clinicians and researchers. Technology is embedded throughout. Clinicians and researchers measure every aspect of patients' activities to mine data that improves outcomes and enables researchers to learn and share new insights in real time.

The patient experience has multiple touchpoints and extends from the entrance to the patient rooms. This experience is manifested through the design—from the extra wide corridors, curved at every corner for better sight lines and mobility, to optimized spaces that communicate wellness. Access to natural light is maximized. Landscaping and green space afford access to gardens for respite.

Foro Boca Concert Hall
Boca del Río, Mexico
Rojkind Arquitectos

TYPE
CONCEPTS — PLUS:
ARCHITECTURE +
URBAN TRANSFORMATION

DETAILS — PLUS:
ARCHITECTURE + CONCRETE

WINNER
JURY

PROJECT STATUS
BUILT

YEAR
2017

FIRM LOCATION
MEXICO CITY
MEXICO

The then mayor of Boca del Río, Mexico, asked Rojkind Arquitectos to design a home for the philharmonic orchestra. The chosen site was located in a deteriorated area of Boca del Río where the Jamapa River meets the Gulf of Mexico. The aim was to make sure that the public spaces were considered as important as the building, giving back to the community by extending the plazas toward the beach, the breakwater, and the city.

The raw grandeur of the exterior is carried into the interiors, expressed as soaring voids. Visitors enter the building beneath a cantilevered corner block, which hovers above the new public plaza. Inside, the main lobby is daylit from skylights above and animated by suspended bridges and stairs that crisscross the space to flow to the auditorium's different access points.

Appropriating the language of the jetty's crude concrete blocks, the building was conceived as a cluster of cubelike volumes to break down its 58,000-square-foot (5,390 square meters) mass. Inside, the design includes a 966-seat performance hall surrounded by back-of-house functions, as well as rehearsal rooms and other spaces that can host additional cultural programs.

Crossroads Garden Shed
Calgary, AB, Canada
5468796 Architecture

TYPE
CONCEPTS — PLUS:
ARCHITECTURE + URBAN
TRANSFORMATION

WINNER
POPULAR CHOICE

PROJECT STATUS
BUILT

YEAR
2017

FIRM LOCATION
WINNIPEG, MB
CANADA

The Crossroads Garden Shed demonstrates the capacity of architecture to transform communities with even the smallest of briefs, thereby affirming its value. Intended to supply a growing neighborhood with a simple storage structure for gardening tools and outdoor furniture, the original vision shifted drastically when reapproached as a unique opportunity to enhance the pedestrian realm.

As inherently stable and waterproof structures, three shipping containers establish the base structure. Selected for their utilitarian nature, and in response to the brief and budget, the containers were placed to create intimate spaces within the overall structure, which acts as a threshold between the street, play area, and gardens. One container is used as a tool shed, while the remaining two provide programmable space and additional storage.

The containers are made of Cor-Ten steel, making them a natural choice for the whole structure. Their corrugated geometry is multiplied and stretched through layering Cor-Ten plates and expanded metal mesh, consequently softening the structure's appearance. An oblong grid of hexagonal Cor-Ten shapes creates a domed surface to gather within; steel honeycombs open skyward in vertical flues and— connected by an overhead trellis— dapple the ground below with light.

Vieira de Almeida & Associados New Headquarters
Lisbon, Portugal

OPENBOOK Architecture
and PMC Arquitectos

TYPE
CONCEPTS — PLUS:
ARCHITECTURE + WORK SPACE

WINNER
JURY
POPULAR CHOICE

PROJECT STATUS
BUILT

YEAR
2017

FIRM LOCATION
LISBON
PORTUGAL

The building is located in one of the trendiest areas of Lisbon. It is a property with essentially industrial characteristics, which originally housed a foundry and was later occupied by an automobile dealer.

The philosophy of intervention was based on the maintenance of the exterior, endowing the contemporary interior with a surprise effect. The atrium is distributed across three distinct zones: the historical nucleus, called the Forum by the occupant, an auditorium inside the atrium, and finally, the work zones.

The work areas occupy the largest floor space in the office. They are developed horizontally, over three floors, with vertical communication atriums. The introduction of natural light in the spaces—through large skylights along the body of the building—guarantees adequate environmental quality.

The building features a large social area where the bar and cafeteria assume the main role. An exterior balcony on the first-floor level completes the space. In terms of materiality, the use of steel, glass, and concrete, together with the traditional wood and carpet, allowed for the creation of an image that appropriates the concept of industrial rehabilitation.

Joseph D. Jamail Lecture Hall
New York, NY, USA

LTL Architects

TYPE
DETAILS — PLUS:
ARCHITECTURE + ACOUSTICS

WINNER
JURY

PROJECT STATUS
BUILT

YEAR
2017

FIRM LOCATION
NEW YORK, NY
USA

For this important lecture space in McKim, Mead & White's historic Pulitzer Hall at Columbia University's School of Journalism, the design was intentionally developed to have a dual personality. To accommodate the broad range of functions required, from lectures to classes to film screenings, the plan is open to multiple configurations via a series of mobile furniture components, including a transformable stage and a moving storage wall. By contrast, the renovated ceiling is highly articulated; developed to function as a contour of performance, with custom panels that provide for lighting, mechanical systems, and acoustics.

The custom ceiling deploys digital fabrication techniques to translate the historical architecture of the coffer into a complex functional surface, formed from recycled acoustical felt modules and shaped to incorporate all of the space's technical systems, from diffusers to a large-scale cinematic projector.

The shape of the ceiling is adjusted to allow for views to the monumental windows and extends to the surface of the mezzanine at the back of the space, referencing the form of classical coffers while adapting to contemporary requirements. While the floor reflects the building's original architecture and materiality, it also acts as a kind of game board for new forms of collectivity and collaboration.

Mead Johnson Nutrition
Chicago, IL, USA

Arktura and Partners by Design

Arktura and Partners by Design collaborated on Mead Johnson Nutrition's new 62,000-square-foot (5,760 square meters) North America headquarters in Chicago to create a customized organic acoustic ceiling that helps bring in the outside, blending naturalistic beauty and functionality. It enhances the space while serving as an expression of its surroundings and the client's corporate culture and values.

The space takes cues from water to reflect its location at the foot of the Chicago River where its three branches meet and—because of its strong ties to life—is a fit for Mead Johnson's corporate mission to nourish the world's children. Constructed of flowing acoustical planes that undulate organically across the floor plan, its tailor-made natural acoustic ceiling system, fabricated by Arktura, ties together the space's atrium and hallways, dampening noise while reinforcing the sense of fluid motion of water below.

Its baffles are constructed from Arktura's high-performance Soft Sound acoustical material, made from 100 percent recyclable PET and NRC rated up to 0.9, allowing the ceiling to achieve significant noise reduction throughout the space. It successfully conveys naturalism through both its form and surface, thanks to utilization of a wood texture variation of Arktura's Soft Sound that mimics light oak.

TYPE
DETAILS — PLUS:
ARCHITECTURE + ACOUSTICS

WINNER
POPULAR CHOICE

PROJECT STATUS
BUILT

YEAR
2017

FIRM LOCATION
GARDENA
PORTUGAL

Shui Cultural Center
Sandu Shui County, China

West-line Studio

TYPE
DETAILS — PLUS:
ARCHITECTURE + CONCRETE

WINNER
POPULAR CHOICE

PROJECT STATUS
BUILT

YEAR
2017

FIRM LOCATION
GUIYANG
CHINA

Located in the southern Guizhou Province, China, this cultural center is a gateway to the land of the Shui. The Shui are one of the ethnic minority groups in China who still retain their own language, together with their unique system of pictographs.

The site, which covers an area of 148,541 square feet (13,800 square meters), was created by a bend in the river and is surrounded by water on three sides. On the west side, a water square welcomes the visitors. *Shui* means "water," which is why this element is so relevant for both the site and project.

The building itself consists of three main stripes, which combine all functions of a tourism-and-culture center. The ritual hall is characterized by sharp edges, strong colors, and a narrow space, aiming to create a strong first impression on visitors. The second stripe still keeps the sharp roof but welcomes visitors with less dramatic tones and serves as a reception hall. On the ground level of the third stripe, the pitch roof is lost in order to find a more conventional space that includes all the main functions: visitor and service center, cafeteria, restrooms, business center, and an upstairs office area.

Kanda Terrace
Tokyo, Japan

Key Operation Inc. / Architects

Located in a central Tokyo neighborhood with many office buildings, this rental building for restaurants stands on a long, narrow lot, surrounded by streets on three sides. Particular attention has been given to the facade of the new building. It features a recessed facade with 3-D stacked terraces. The size and shape of these terraces vary from floor to floor, creating a layered form that changes as it moves upward.

Entirely made of glass, the dynamic facade allows people to look into the restaurants. The undersides of the protruding spaces and terraces—very exposed to passersby—are finished with a smoked, white ash wooden cladding, highlighted by the black joinery work of the building. Because of its location in the city center, the mid-rise building needed to be commercially efficient, occupying the entire permissible floor-area ratio and opening the space to restaurant visitors on every floor. It was therefore essential to create an alluring image of a building filled with restaurants and to set up a bright, welcoming environment for visitors. In response to its context, the building, like a porous volume, encourages terraces on each floor to connect to the street and its larger neighborhood.

TYPE
DETAILS – PLUS:
ARCHITECTURE + FACADES

WINNER
POPULAR CHOICE

PROJECT STATUS
BUILT

YEAR
2017

FIRM LOCATION
TOKYO
JAPAN

Efjord
Ballangen, Norway

Stinessen Arkitektur

The clients desired a retreat that focused on the panoramic views of the site, but also transported them to a feeling of isolation and total privacy, away from hectic workdays in the city. The conceptual layout opens and closes the building in different directions; the eastern part of the cabin closes toward some neighboring buildings and opens toward a ridge; the opposite directions are sought at the front end of the cabin, opening up to the magnificent views toward the dramatic mountains and the fjord to the west.

The two volumes are slightly offset to provide for sheltered outdoor areas and views towards the fjord also from the rear volume. The terrain itself provided a perfectly natural orientation of the building that allows the different functions to work in tune with the movement of the sun and the balance between privacy and views.

The exterior of the cabin consists of two materials, structural glazing and core pinewood. The wood is treated with iron sulfate to achieve an even patina. The interiors are clad in birch veneer and the floors in tiles of granite, the stone outside. Both types of wood are typical for this region.

TYPE
DETAILS — PLUS:
ARCHITECTURE + GLASS

WINNER
POPULAR CHOICE

PROJECT STATUS
BUILT

YEAR
2017

FIRM LOCATION
TROMSØ
NORWAY

Green Places
Community Clubhouse
Tainan, Taiwan

Chain10 Architecture
and Interior Design Institute

This building located in Tainan, Taiwan, provides spaces for dining, reading, exercising, learning, sharing, and communicating for local residents. The design is based on natural patterns and includes a reflecting pond and outdoor plaza, as well as offering unobstructed views of the nearby hills. The floors are stacked vertically as a series of free curves. Varied surfaces with differing heights provide an opportunity for enhanced interaction between visitors. Natural elements are brought into the building not only through its decor, but also with a wall formed of tall trees.

The use of continuous glass windows breaks spatial barriers, thereby inviting nature indoors and creating links between the inside and the outside. The walls contain anodized aluminum and an RC layer; cold air flows through

the layers for cooling in summer months. In winter, the design, large trees, double walls, and other elements effectively block cold air from entering inside.

Eco-friendly, recyclable building materials were selected to reduce replacement rates and decrease the impact on the environment. Another important factor is the use of integrated angles made from materials such as aluminum, metal, and types of glass with good longevity and weather resistance. Renewable power generated from solar energy completes the building's goal to function as sustainably as possible.

TYPE
DETAILS — PLUS:
ARCHITECTURE + METAL

WINNER
JURY
POPULAR CHOICE

PROJECT STATUS
BUILT

YEAR
2015

FIRM LOCATION
KAOHSIUNG
TAIWAN

VOA Space
Khon Kaen, Thailand

Ekaphap Duangkaew, EKAR,
Creative and Design Office,
Interiors by Kittinut Thamrak

VOA Space appears as a visually striking structure. Its presence stands out from the surrounding context of the city, particularly in an area predominantly occupied by shop windows and car showrooms. Part of its architectural makeup consists of a wall of concrete laths. Clad with tiles, the wall merges with the remaining columns, beams, and the roof structure of the original building.

Utilizing architectural compositions to facilitate functional spaces and activities, the formality of a commercial showroom is converged with the functionality of a working area that can also inspire creativity.

This image favored a building where new and old elements meet to mingle. The tile-clad concrete wall unites itself with the old building's existing structure in places where original walls have been torn down. The new wall encloses the space and divides the functional area into two zones; a boundary between each zone is obscured by the presence of the concrete lath wall with a landscape in the middle, linking the interior spaces together.

An elevated walkway connects the spaces on the upper floor with an airy mass between the lath walls that not only softens the dividing line between the two areas, but also blurs the physical boundary between the program's interior and exterior.

TYPE
DETAILS — PLUS:
ARCHITECTURE + STAIRS

WINNER
JURY

PROJECT STATUS
BUILT

YEAR
2018

FIRM LOCATION
BANGKOK
THAILAND

Temple in Stone and Light
Barmer, India
SpaceMatters

Located in the culturally rich area of Rajasthan, the project was an opportunity to explore and establish contemporary interpretations of traditional typologies and building techniques. The contextual response to the region's architecture rendered a design that sought to reinvent the boundaries of modern temple architecture.

The decision to use stone masonry was an attempt to pay homage to the region's building style and yet provide novelty in a temple of that region. Considering the setting of the temple in the wonderfully stark and alive canvas of the Thar desert, the primary building material was the yellow, locally available Jaisalmer sandstone. The main innovation is in the *shikhar*—the temple's rising tower—which is supported by solid dressed stone masonry.

The massive stone masonry walls designed to hold the stone shikhar had to be placed precisely to balance the various requirements. The interlocking stone joinery was employed to let light into the inner sanctum, or *garbhagriha*, of the temple during the day and let light out during the night, transforming the temple from day to night. At different times of the day, from different directions, the temple is heavy and light, solid and translucent, solid and void, past and present.

TYPE
DETAILS — PLUS:
ARCHITECTURE + STONE

WINNER
JURY

PROJECT STATUS
BUILT

YEAR
2015

FIRM LOCATION
DELHI
INDIA

Chetian Cultural Center
Chetian Village, China

West-line Studio

This cultural center is located in the rural Chetian Village in the Guizhou Province in southwest China. The village has more than four hundred years of history and is famous for its stone houses. Forty-one families, out of the 207 living in the village, belong to the Miao ethnic minority, one of the oldest minority groups in China.

The architecture of the cultural center is characterized by thick walls, built with the stone from the village's pit. The stone has a unique blue shade, which is why it is commonly called the "blue stone." It originates from sedimentary rocks, with major components being limestone and dolomite. The designers studied the existing stone houses of the village in order to preserve the traditional masonry methods, together with more modern construction technologies.

The result is a series of trials, mistakes, and irregularities, which deliberately become an active part of the architecture, because each and every stone keeps the memory of its construction process and of the different hands of those who have shaped it. The strong presence of the stone creates an intimate interior space and shows the architects' deep respect for the historical masonry traditions and culture of southwest China stone villages.

TYPE
DETAILS — PLUS:
ARCHITECTURE + STONE

WINNER
POPULAR CHOICE

PROJECT STATUS
BUILT

YEAR
2015

FIRM LOCATION
GUIYANG
CHINA

Index

Page references for illustrations appear in **bold** type.

Photography Credits

Every reasonable effort has been made to acknowledge the ownership of copyright for photographs included in this volume. Any errors that may have occurred are inadvertent and will be corrected in subsequent editions, provided notification is sent in writing to the publisher.

Front and back covers: Aldo Amoretti.

Patrick Tourneboeuf: 12–13; Chen Hao: 14–15; Nic Lehoux: 16; Aleksandar Vrzalski/Vrzalski Photography: 17; Hufton+Crow: 18–21, 46–47, 134, 223; K. Taro Hashimura / Hashi Studio: 22; David Rahr: 23; Tim Griffith: 24–25; Aedas: 26–29; Ligang Huang: 30–33; Prue Ruscoe: 34–35 (t); Ben Hosking: 35 (b); Ossip van Duivenbode: 36, 112–115; Doublespace Photography: 37, 114; XIA Zhi: 38–39; Saeid Faramarzi: 40–41; Bruce Damonte: 42–43, 160–163; Yugon Kim: 44; Hiroyuki Oki / Decon Photo Studio: 45; Rungkit Charoenwat: 48–51; Fran Parente: 52; HDR: 53; BAD. Built by Associative Data: 54; Jin Weiqi: 55; Enrique Avilés: 56–57; Ema Peter: 58–59, 228 (b); Changhae Studio: 60; STUDIO SQUARE: 61; Mark Williams: 62–67; Paul Quiambao: 68; Casey Dunn: 69–71; Schran Image: 72–73; João Morgado: 74, 229 (b); LUXIGON: 75; Aesthetica Studio: 76–77; Tihomir Rachev / One Eye Production: 78; NAARO: 79–81; Miran Kambič: 82; David Sundberg / ESTO: 83; Emily Tang Spear: 84; Fan Wang: 85; Irina Boersma / Studio David Thulstrup: 86; ZHANG Dengxing: 87; BNS studio: 88; W Workspace: 89–93, 196; Fernando Alda: 94–97; de Leon & Primmer Architecture Workshop: 98–99; Edwin Seda: 100–105; Su Shengliang: 106-109; Mr. Albert Lim K.S.: 110–111; Mohammad Reza Hoorjandi: 116; Paul Dyer Photography: 117–118; Marion Brenner Photography: 119–120; Diana Cheren Nygren: 121–122; Leon Alexander Single: 123; Ranjith Akkarathodi: 124; OMA + OLIN: 125–129; IF (Integrated Field): 130; Felix Forest: 131; Pedro Kok: 132–133; Ewout Huibers: 135–137; Peter Bennetts: 138–139; Shannon McGrath: 140–141; Lucas K. Doolan / Studio Millspace: 142–143; George Messaritakis: 144, 147; decaARCHITECTURE: 145–146; Fernando Guerra / FG+SG: 148-151, 158–159; Naho Kubota: 152–153; Nguyen Tien Thanh: 154–155; Paul Rivera: 156–157, 244–245, 247; Rafael Gamo: 164–167; Tom Arban Photography: 168; Terje Arntsen: 169–171; Ehsan Karimi / Esun Studio: 172; Ernesto Vela: 173; estudio santander: 174 (t); Monk Mackenzie Architects: 174 (b), 191 (t); Eco Arch-VIz Studio: 175 (t); PARA: 175 (b); hes.architects: 176; Rasmus Hjortshoj / COAST: 177; Alberto Cosi: 178–181; Aldo Amoretti: 182–183; Light Earth Designs: 184–185; Jonathan Gregson for Yorkshire Tea: 186–187; Octav Tirziu: 188; Petra Appelhof Fotografie: 189; John Linden: 190; GOA: 191 (b); Alexandre Zveiger: 192–195; Iwan Baan: 197–201; Jeremy Bittermann / Joel B Sanders Agency: 202–207; YANG Chaoying: 208; Dinesh Mehta: 209-211; Matthew Mazzotta: 212; Aidin Gilandoost: 213; Soroush Majidi: 214; Studio TM: 215; Damir Fabijanic: 216; Kathrine Sørgård: 217-219; Kenrick Wong / Magic Kwan: 220; Onnis Luque / Yupica: 221; HG Esch: 222, 224–225; Jeroen Musch Photography: 226; Kasita: 227; Brick Visual: 228 (t); John Linden: 229 (t); Xufeng Jing Studio: 230–235; Deimel + Wittmar: 236–237; Anotherspacestudio and Sofography: 238–241; Xing Fu / Fuxing Architecture Photo Studio: 242; Michael Moran / OTTO: 243, 251–253; Jaime Navarro: 246; 5468796 Architecture: 248–249; José Campos: 250; Tom Harris: 254–255; Haobo Wei and Jingsong Xie: 256–259, 272–275; Shigeo Ogawa: 260–261; Steve King: 262–265; Kuo-Min Lee: 266–267; Chalermwat Wongchompoo: 268–269; Akash Das: 210–271.

Acknowledgments

Colophon

This book is dedicated to the world's architects.

Thank you to the Architizer team, with a special
thanks to Nikki-Lee Birdsey, Kelly Britton, Paul Keskeys,
Joanna Kloppenburg, and Chloé Vadot.

Phaidon Press Limited
Regent's Wharf
All Saints Street
London N1 9PA

Phaidon Press Inc.
65 Bleecker Street
New York, NY 10012

phaidon.com

First published 2019
© 2019 Phaidon Press Limited

ISBN 978 0 7148 7870 6

A CIP catalogue record for this book is available from
the British Library and the Library of Congress.

Commissioning Editor: Emilia Terragni
Project Editor: François-Luc Giraldeau
Production Controller: Lisa Fiske
Design: Nicholas Stover, Order

Printed in China